Dinghies

and

Daysailers

THE Guide To Nearly 200 Non-Cabin Sailboats
From 6 Feet To 38 Feet. Over 300 Photos and
Drawings. Prices – Specifications – Histories –
Ratings – Addresses – and Telephone Numbers

BUTCH & RITA WILCOX

 Barca De Vela Publishing, Phoenix, Arizona

Dinghies and Daysailers

THE Guide To Nearly 200 Non-Cabin Sailboats From 6 Feet To 38 Feet. Over 300 Photos and Drawings. Prices – Specifications – Histories – Ratings – Addresses – and Telephone Numbers

By Butch & Rita Wilcox

Published by:

Barca De Vela Publishing
Post Office Box 37618
Phoenix, Arizona 85069-7168 U.S.A.

Library of Congress Cataloging in Publication Data.
Wilcox, Butch, 1942-
   Dinghies and daysailers.

   Includes index.
   1. Sailboats--Catalogs. I. Wilcox, Rita,
1948-   . II. Title.
VM351.W53   1987   623.8'223'0294   87-22354
ISBN 0-944236-39-1 (pbk.)

ACKNOWLEDGEMENT

We have not attempted to cite all of the authorities and sources consulted in preparing this book. To do so would require more space than is available.

Many people contributed their time and efforts to this book. We want to extend a special thanks to all of the class associations, manufacturers and their representatives.

We express our thanks to the United States Naval Institute for their permission to reprint selected prayers taken from **PRAYERS AT SEA**, by Chaplain Joseph F. Parker.

Lee Parks, of the United States Yacht Racing Union; and Ann Wells, of Small Boat Journal, gave us great guidance and encouragement throughout the entire process.

We sincerely thank all of these people for the part they played in the development of this book. We also thank them for helping to spread the word about all the fine boats available to those who are interested in the great sport of sailing.

Cover by Denise Milner

WARNING -- DISCLAIMER

This book is designed to provide information in regard to the subject matter covered. It is not the purpose of this book to reprint all the information that is otherwise available to the authors and/or publisher, but to compliment, amplify and supplement other information sources. For more information, contact the manufacturers and class associations listed in the book.

Every effort has been made to make this book as complete and as accurate as possible. However, there may be mistakes, both typographical and in content. Therefore, this text should be used only as a general guide and not as the ultimate source of information on dinghies and daysailers. Furthermore, this book contains information on dinghies and daysailers only up to the printing date.

The purpose of this book is to educate and entertain. The authors and Barca De Vela Publishing shall have neither liability nor responsibility to any person or entity with respect to any loss or damage caused or alleged to be caused directly or indirectly by the information contained in this book.

WARNING -- DISCLAIMER

TABLE OF CONTENTS

ALL WE WANTED WAS A SAILBOAT

The intent of **DINGHIES AND DAYSAILERS** is to provide a directory of sailboats being manufactured for those of us who **just want to SAIL**. This book was borne out of our own search for a new boat. After sailing for a few years and having owned some of the more recognized daysailers, we were interested in getting into a littler larger family daysailer/racer. We didn't want a cabin, nor porta-potti, nor sleeping quarters, nor cooking facilities, nor any of the other extras needed for spending the night. We just wanted to **Go Sailing** -- all we wanted was a **SAILBOAT**. The only information we were able to find locally was from two boat dealers, some magazines and the library. Our efforts here produced very few boats that *might* suit our needs.

While in San Diego on a bare-boat charter, we remembered a fine book store, **Seabreeze Nautical Books And Charts**, that would surely have information on many daysailers, or at least be able to get information for us. The owners helped us find a few books, but each contained information on only a small number of daysailers.

Having been involved in boating for many years, and lived in some major boating areas, we knew there were many fine designs available -- we just had to find them.

With the help of listings from the **United States Yacht Racing Union, Small Boat Journal,** and many other sources across the U.S. and Canada, we were able to find nearly 200 dinghies and daysailers available. After talking with many manufacturers and class representatives, we felt there was a need for a single publication that provided the type of information for which we had been searching.

DINGHIES AND DAYSAILERS is the result of our findings. With each new edition, we hope to add designs we have missed, as well as improve and update information on the boats now included. **We welcome suggestions from YOU** that would help make this book more useful.

How To Use This Book

DINGHIES AND DAYSAILERS can be used for several purposes. It is a great shopping guide for anyone looking for a daysailer, racer or yacht tender. It is also a handy reference book for those of us who are sailing enthusiasts and are always "talking boats".

The information and photos on each boat was obtained from class associations, manufacturers and manufacturer's representatives, with the exception of a few personal experiences. Our draft of each boat represented was forwarded to these individuals to provide them the opportunity to make further suggestions, insure accuracy and fill in any omissions. However, even with great effort to make the information as accurate as possible, mistakes could exist. Some details about specific boats might have changed since the time of our printing. For the very latest information, especially price, be sure to contact the manufacturer.

General Description

Boats are entered by length overall (LOA), beginning with the shortest boat. If you're searching for a specific boat, check the alphabetic Index in the back of the book. If there is a word or term in the description you are not familiar with, check the Glossary, also in the back of the book. Our goal has been to include a description that provides a general "feeling" about the boat, as well as who designed it, a little history, etc. The length of the write-up is a direct result of the amount of information provided. Contact the class or manufacturer for more detailed information on any specific boat.

Class Association

For those boats represented by a class association, we have listed the names of the classes and the addresses to contact for more information. The class can provide information such as: where fleets are located, scheduled events, availability and prices of used boats, and much more valuable information that you might need.

Manufacturer

Addresses and telephone numbers of manufacturers have been included. We attempted to locate every manufacturer of each boat represented. In some cases, we were unable to do so. The manufacturer can help you find a dealer located near you or suggest shipping methods.

Specifications

Specifications will normally list at least the LOA (length overall), Beam (distance across), Weight (or Displacement) of the boat, and total Sail Area. More detailed specifications are listed if they have been provided to us. Contact the class or manufacturer for complete specifications.

Prices

Approximate price, rigged to sail is listed. This does not include trailers (unless so stated) and may not include safety equipment, which may be required by your state or area. Prices can change at any time and may vary from area to area. Prices listed for Canadian manufacturers are, of course, in Canadian currency. Contact the manufacturer for the latest pricing details.

Photos

We used the best photos we could obtain. In some cases, photos were not available. We will continue to pursue more and higher quality photos for future printings.

Portsmouth Yardstick

The Portsmouth Yardstick is a widely used method of rating boats of different classes racing on the same course. The rating is derived from actual racing experience. By comparing Portsmouth numbers, one can get an idea of relative speed potential of the boat/class. The lower the number, the faster the boat should be.

The Portsmouth Numbers listed are only the basic numbers and are good for comparison. In actual practice, race committees can adjust these up or down for wind conditions and other factors. For a complete listing, contact the United States Yacht Racing Union.

A list of those boats with Portsmouth Numbers can be found in the back of the book in the Appendix - Portsmouth Numbers.

PHRF Handicaps

PHRF Handicap is a "seconds-per-mile" handicap system, which also allows different classes to compete on the same course. The handicap is multiplied by the course distance in miles to give the "time allowance" for the race. Corrected time is simply "finish time" minus "time allowance".

PHRF Handicaps can vary slightly from area to area. The handicaps listed were calculated by averaging all areas reporting handicaps to the USYRU. For a complete listing of PHRF Handicaps, contact the USYRU.

A listing of the boats with PHRF Handicaps can be found in the back of the book in the Appendix - PHRF Handicaps.

Prayers At Sea

Throughout this book you will notice several prayers. These were taken from **PRAYERS AT SEA**, by Chaplain Joseph F. Parker, reprinted by permission of the United States Naval Institute. Parker was commissioned a Chaplain in the U.S. Navy in April 1941. During the 24 years in the Armed Forces he served aboard the USS Chaumont, a transport, and two Essex class aircraft carriers, the USS Hancock and the USS Tarawa. He served with the Marines in Korea. He was awarded thirteen campaign ribbons and medals and is the recipient of a "Personal Letter of Commendation with Medal."

Boats Not Included

If your favorite dinghy or daysailer is not listed in this book, and is being manufactured today, contact and send information to: Barca De Vela Publishing, P.O. Box 37168, Phoenix, Arizona 85069-7168.

Happy Reading

DINGHIES AND DAYSAILERS /

6' To 10.99'

TADPOLE

It's a "Boat In A Box"! You open the box and find absolutely everything: pre-cut Marine ply, epoxy, pre-made rudder, centerboard case, beautiful wooden oars, sails, rigging, brass hardware, color coded manual, and even tools! Its innovative construction means that it can be assembled in an hour and completed in an easy and pleasant weekend.

We're talking about the 6' **TADPOLE** with a gaff rig. This little boat can be carried on the shoulder and car-topped easily...and *wheeled*. That's right, there's a wheel at the front and cunning handles at the back. So, pushing is a *pushover*. Just throw in your tackle and supplies and roll it down to the water.

Folks who would never dream of building a boat can actually build a **TADPOLE** in a weekend. Once she's finished, the traditional design, durability, beauty and flexibility of this sweet-looking pram are constant reminders that there is nothing quite like Merryman's "Boat In A Box".

Manufacturer:
Merryman Boats,
The Boat In A
Box, 127 W.
North St., Ithaca,
Michigan 48847.
517/875-3788

SPECIFICATIONS:
TADPOLE
LOA: 6'
Width: 3'6"
Weight: 45 lbs.
Sail Area: 30 s.f.

Approximate
Price:
Sail - $599
Row - $499

MONTGOMERY DINGHY

A proper dinghy must do several things well. It must row easily, sail, and handle a small outboard. It must be light enough to be handled easily but strong enough to withstand hard use. It must be fine forward to row well and sail upwind, but have plenty of reserve buoyancy for the sake of safety. It must be dry and secure in a chop but without excessive freeboard or it won't row against a strong head wind. A sailing dinghy must have a strong but simple rig that is easily stored and rigged, and must sail well in order to double as a trainer and as The Kid's Boat.

MONTGOMERY 6'8"

Since 1969, cruising yachtsmen have considered the **MONTGOMERY** yacht tenders to be the very finest. They fulfill all the requirements of a dinghy with class and style. They are very well finished and perform like

MONTGOMERY DINGHY

no others. The hand laminated glasswork is complemented by rails, transoms, and mast partners of oiled teak. The lapstrake hulls are based on traditional designs that have proven themselves over many decades. The interior finish is Gelcoat, which will withstand the passage of time and makes bonded repairs simple. All joiner work is glued with Urac, bedded in polysulphide, and fastened with stainless. Oar sockets, lifting eyes, tiller straps, towing eyes, and leeboard brackets are of cast bronze.

The mast is tapered fiberglass, 13'3" long, and optionally available in a two-piece version. The aluminum boom folds up against the mast without removing the gooseneck. Rudders, leeboards, and daggerboards are varnished mahogany; tillers are oiled teak.

The **MONTGOMERY** sailing models come in three sizes -- the 6-8 (shown in photo), the 7-11 and the 9. The 6-8 is a pram and has a tremendous amount of buoyancy. The 7-11 and 9 are available with either leeboard or daggerboard.

Manufacturer: Montgomery Marine Products, 3236 Fitzgerald Road, #I, Rancho Cordova, CA 95670. 916/635-3158

SPECIFICATIONS: MONTGOMERY DINGHY 6-8
LOA: 6'8", Beam: 3'10", Weight: 74 lbs.

Approximate Price: 6-8 $975, 7-11 $1185, 9 $1295.

Our gracious Father, everywhere all great men have been servants. We pray that we may be most anxious to help others before self, to serve and not to be served. We are not charged by Thee to be successful but to do our best with the task that is set before us. Help us to be good shipmates that the end of the day may find us unashamed. Amen.

FATTY KNEES

The famous **FATTY KNEES** dinghy, designed by Lyle C. Hess, is offered in 7', 8' and 9' models (7-foot shown in photo). They cartop nicely and are light enough to handle on/off board for cruising. Their great capacity means less trips ashore or when laying at anchor.

The name "Fatty Knees" is appropriate, with its wide beam relative to length. The name came from a time Lyle's wife, Doodle, was drying their three year old granddaughter after a bath. Doodle squeezed one of the child's knees and said, "Lamb, you've got fatty knees". Lamb then reached over and took hold of one of Doodle's knees and retorted, "Grandma, you *really* got fatty knees".

The list of design features is extensive including strong lapstrake hull, finely finished inside and out, double teal gunwales, teak knees, mahogany rudder and board, and Sitka spruce boom. The **FATTY KNEES** features a unique detachable gooseneck, which allows roller reefing the sail by rotating the mast.

The **FATTY KNEES** offers smart sailing, easy rowing and polite towing, along with great capacity and outstanding stability.

Manufacturer: Grace Marine Corp., 200 Corporate Place, Suite 7, Peabody, MA 01960-3828. 617/535-7748

SPECIFICATIONS: FATTY KNEES
7-Foot LOA: 7', Beam: 4', Weight: 70 lbs., Max. H.P.: 2, Capacity: 500 lbs.

8-Foot LOA: 8', Beam: 4'3", Weight: 80 lbs., Max. H.P.: 2, Capacity: 750 lbs.

9-Foot LOA: 9', Beam, 4'6", Weight: 90 lbs., Max. H.P.: 2, Capacity: 850 lbs.

Approximate Price: Range $1400 to $2500.

FATTY KNEES

Fatty Knees 7'

SEA WITCH

This 7' hard chine dinghy is easy to rig and a delight to sail. Just slip the mast into the sail sleeve, step, and away you go. The **SEA WITCH** has dual rowing positions, Dacron sail, two-piece anodized mast and boom, mahogany rudder and daggerboard, oak tiller and all stainless hardware.

Every Ensign Dinghy is built to the high quality standards of Mike Dapice, founder of Ensign Dinghies and Marine. Coremat construction assures strength as well as a lightweight hull. All hull fittings are backed by hardwood plates. Seats are molded in or solid mahogany. Interior and exterior is gelcoated for beauty as well as easy cleanup.

Manufacturer: Ensign Dinghies & Marine, Michael Dapice Enterprises, Inc., P.O. Box 547, Rye, NY 10580. 914/967-1656

SPECIFICATIONS:
SEA WITCH
LOA: 7'
Beam: 4'1"
Depth: 17"
Sail Area: 36 s.f.
Weight: 75 lbs.
Capacity: 375 lbs.
Max. H.P.: 2.

Approximate
Price: $690.

18

L DINGHY

The new **Sumner L DINGHY** offers a full internal liner bonded to the hull. This creates a boat of unmatched strength and beauty.

The **L DINGHY** has a hard chine, a deep underwater configuration and a long deep skeg. These insure ease of boarding, as well as stability at sea.

At **Sumner**, they build their lifeboat Dinghies with lift-out seats and side flotation chambers. In rough water, when the crew is seated high on fixed seats, they are top-heavy and will capsize...not so with these boats!

Rowing the **L DINGHY** maintains their tradition of excellence in rowing and towing. Multiple rowing stations and movable seats insure level fore and aft trim, regardless of loading. The skeg is deep and long for efficient tracking. The tow-eye is positioned low so the bow will not dig in while under tow.

Sailing the **L DINGHY** is a snap. She can be converted from a rowing dinghy to a sailboat in seconds. She comes with a modern gunter rig and features functional leeboards, which provide stability without the need of a trunk cluttering the middle of the boat.

The **L DINGHY** is available in 7' and 8' models (7-foot shown in photo). She is light weight and has a specially designed gunwale, which permits a good grasp. The inner gel coat finish resists soiling so that the boat maintains its beauty for years. She also has ample dry storage forward in a watertight compartment. Fine craftsmanship, beautiful design and quality...the **L DINGHY**.

Manufacturer: Sumner Boat Company, Inc., 334 S. Bayview Avenue, Amityville, NY 11701. 516/264-1830

SPECIFICATIONS: 7' L DINGHY
LOA: 7'2", Beam: 4'2", Depth: 18", Weight: 75 lbs., Weight Capacity: 470 lbs., Persons Capacity: 398 lbs., Sail Area: 35 s.f., Max. H.P.: 2 **Approximate Price:** Row: $549, Sail: $829.

L DINGHY

7' L DINGHY

OPTIMIST

The **OPTIMIST** is really divided into two classes, the **Dinghy** and the **Pram** associations. The original was designed in Clearwater, Florida in 1947 by Clark Mills for members of a Youth Club that had been fitting sails to soap-boxes and racing in the street.

OPTIMIST DINGHY

The **OPTIMIST PRAM** spread quickly in America. There are two versions as to how the **OPTIMIST DINGHY** class developed. One is that a Danish architect, Axel Damgaard read about the **PRAM** in an American magazine and with friends in the Vordingborg Sailing Club, built some for a youth program in Denmark and soon spread in Europe. The other version is that some British officers making port in Miami in the 50's were invited to the Coral Reef Yacht Club and after having a few, competed with some of the members in their youth program **PRAMS** and were so impressed, they took plans back to England and the design spread from there.

OPTIMIST

In either case, the **OPTIMIST** soon became extremely popular in Europe and the U.S. The European **OPTIMIST** somehow ended up about 7 lbs. heavier than the original **PRAM** and had slightly more sail area. Either boat is a fine youth boat. In 1965 in Finland, the International **Optimist Dinghy** Association was formed and has grown to over 130,000 and is the world's largest class in the International Yacht Racing Union. The Original **Optimist Pram** Association is still in Florida, but has not grown like the European boat.

Class Association - Pram: Clearwater Optimist Pram Class Association, P.O. Box 547, Largo, FL 33540.

Class Association - Dinghy: U.S. Optimist Dinghy Association, P.O. Box 330971, Miami, FL 33133-0971.

Manufacturer's Rep.: Optimist USA, Inc., 154 N. Fair Street, P.O. Box 394, Guilford, CT 06437. 203/453-0504

SPECIFICATIONS: OPTIMIST

Pram: LOA: 7'6.5", Beam: 3'8.5", Sail Area: 35 s.f., Hull Weight: 70 lbs.

Dinghy: LOA: 7'8", Beam: 3'8", Sail Area: 35 s.f., Hull Weight: 77 lbs.

Approximate Price: Dinghy $1395.

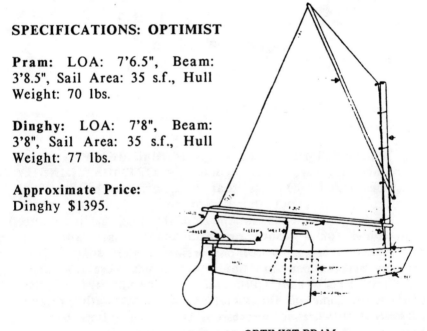

OPTIMIST PRAM

BAUER 8

The **BAUER 8**, designed by Hans- Christof Bauer, is Bauteck Marine's newest addition to their dinghy line.

This dinghy accommodates the cruiser with limited deck space, but still provides maximum loading capacity and sailing performance.

Made of hand-laid fiberglass, its foam core makes it truly unsinkable. The **BAUER 8** is available in row or sail models. She can be purchased as a hull, kit or fully completed.

Manufacturer: Bauteck Marine Corp., Inc., 88 South Dixie Highway, St. Augustine, Florida 32084. 904/824-8826

SPECIFICATIONS:
BAUER 8
LOA: 7'9"
Beam: 49"
Height: 21"

Approximate Price:
From $500 to $1000.

For Thanksgiving Day

Almighty and most merciful Father, from whom cometh every good and perfect gift; we give Thee hearty thanks for all Thy goodness unto us. Thou hast filled the sea and land with plenty that no man should go hungry. Help us to share Thy gifts with others. On this day, of all days, we would not forget to offer our gratitude. Amen.

23

NYMPH

This sturdy, good looking dinghy is another of Phil Bolger's designs specifying "tack and tape" construction which cuts costs and is ideal for the amateur builder. This is a very good rowing or sailing dinghy.

Harold H. "Dynamite" Payson offers the **NYMPH** ready to sail or will sell plans for $20.00. Home building cost is approximately $200 and will take 2-3 weeks in your spare time. Harold also offers a new larger version called **RUBEN'S NYMPH**, which looks the same but is a foot wider. He has available approximately 20 other good designs and offers a catalogue of study plans for $3.00.

Manufacturer: Harold H. Payson, Pleasant Beach Road, So. Thomaston, ME 04858. 207/594-7887

SPECIFICATIONS: NYMPH
LOA: 7'9", Beam: 3'6", Weight: 63 lbs. **Approx. Price:** $950.

FROG

Here's another "Boat In A Box"! -- from Merryman Boats. Just like **Tadpole**, her baby sister, the **FROG** has absolutely everything: pre-cut Marine ply, epoxy, pre-made rudder, centerboard case, beautiful wooden oars, sails, rigging, brass hardware, color coded manual, and even tools! Its innovative construction means that it can be assembled in an hour or two and completed in a couple of weekends.

The **FROG** carries a sprit rig and can be carried on the shoulder and car-topped easily...and *wheeled*. There's a wheel at the front and cunning handles at the back. Just throw in your tackle and supplies and roll it down to the water.

FROG

Folks who would never dream of building a boat can actually build a **FROG** in weekend. Once finished, the **FROG**'s traditional design, durability, beauty and flexibility are constant reminders that there is nothing quite like the "Boat In A Box".

Manufacturer: Merryman Boats, The Boat In A Box, 127 W. North St., Ithaca, Michigan 48847. 517/875-3788

SPECIFICATIONS: FROG
LOA: 7'10", Width: 4', Weight: 72 lbs. Sail Area: 40 s.f.

Approximate Price: Sail - $799 Row - $699.

NAPLES SABOT

The first **NAPLES SABOT** was designed and built around 1943 by Roy McCullough and R. A. Violette, in Mr. Violette's garage. They lived in the "Naples" district of Long Beach, California, hence the name. They developed their design from the **Balboa Dinghy** and from a design of the **MacGregor Sabot**. The major change was substituting a leeboard for a centerboard.

The original **NAPLES SABOTS** were built and raced by adults. After official plans were drawn up by L.M. Dingler in 1946, and the numbers of these dinghies grew, children began to race them because of the youth's light weight. And, the kids would regularly outsail the adults! At one point in time, the adults required weights be added to youth boats. Today, the **NAPLES SABOT** is raced in separate classes. There is plenty of competition.

The Naples Sabot Association was founded in 1946, and the class has grown tremendously since then. These are fun little dinghies and make good tenders. You can still build your own from plans supplied by the Class Association ($5.00), or you can purchase from one of the manufacturers.

Class Association: International Naples Sabot Association, Peggy Lenhart, 690 Senate Street, Costa Mesa, CA 92627. 714/645-1245

Manufacturer: Alax Yachts, P.O. Box 83599, San Diego, CA 92138. 619/224-6737

Manufacturer: Corsair/Sher-Fab, 16515 Bellflower Blvd., Bellflower, CA 90706. 213/867-7612

Manufacturer: Mel-Craft, 1835 Whittier Av., F-7, Costa Mesa, CA 92627. 714/642-5195

Manufacturer: International Sailing Products - West, 412 29th St., Newport Beach, CA 92663. 714/673-5774

SPECIFICATIONS: NAPLES SABOT
LOA: 7'10", Beam: 3'10", Sail Area: 38 s.f., Weight: 95 lbs.

Approximate Price: $1300.

NAPLES SABOT

PUDDLEDUCK

The original **PUDDLEDUCK** was designed by Robert H. Baker in 1951 and was built for the student's sailing and racing program at St. George's School in Portsmouth, Rhode Island.

PUDDLEDUCK's beauty lies in her versatility. She can either be rowed, sailed or motored. The dinghy is light and exceedingly stout. It's an ideal sailing dinghy for children as well as adults - generous beam, a hard chine and a small sail area gives the **PUDDLEDUCK** great stability with outstanding maneuverability.

Due to the **PUDDLEDUCK**'s V-bottom with more than the usual dead-rise, sheer and rocker, the dinghy is endowed with excellent sailing characteristics and is a proven four-knot sailer. Unique side-thwart seating provides additional, dry seating to make sailing more comfortable for adults as well as children.

PUDDLEDUCK's excellent towing characteristics are due to her light weight, low-placed tow ring, and deep skeg which offers virtually no resistance. Positive flotation allows her to be Coast Guard rated for three people or 390 lbs. and a 2-horse power out-board motor. Mast components all stow neatly inside the boat, on deck, or in a quarterberth.

Manufacturer: New England Skiff Builders, P.O. Box 267, Wakefield, RI 02880.
401/789-4609

SPECIFICATIONS:
PUDDLEDUCK
LOA: 7'10"
Beam: 4'
Sail Area: 36 s.f.
Weight: 84 lbs.

Approximate Price: $1550

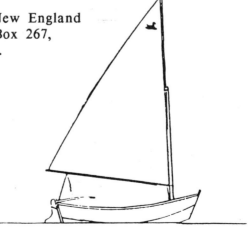

PUDDLEDUCK

PERRYWINKLE 8

This fine little dinghy was originally designed to be tender to the **Valiant 40**. Upon the completion of that project, the **PERRYWINKLE 8** was taken over by a private manufacturing company, initially on the West Coast. Now, the project has moved, and is alive and well in Annapolis, Maryland.

Perrywinkle 8 (far right)

Anyone familiar with Robert Perry's designs will readily recognize the **PERRYWINKLE 8** as the ultimate in classic sailing dinghies.

She is double-ended and has a full-length, ballasted skeg, which makes for great ease in boat sailing, rowing and towing. Constructed using the best of materials and high-quality workmanship, she is stable and easy to maneuver.

PERRYWINKLE 8

PERRYWINKLE 8 is cat-rigged and loose-footed for ease of sailing. She is equipped with the finest quality rigging and sail. Also available in a rowing model, she can be purchased without the teak seatgrates and floorboards.

Built to carry up to 750 pounds, **PERRYWINKLE 8** can handle a maximum 1.5 horsepower engine. She is also available with gunnel guard, motor mount and drain plugs. Her standard hull comes in either white or gray. But for a slight charge, you can have the color you choose including striping.

Manufacturer: Perrywinkle, Inc., Annapolis City Marina, Suite 303, Annapolis, MD 21403. 301/269-0887

Manufacturer: Luna Yachts, Ltd., Unit 20, 427 Speers Road, Oakville, Ontario, Canada L6K 3S8. 416/842-4808

SPECIFICATIONS: PERRYWINKLE 8
LOA: 7'11", LWL: 7'2", Beam: 4', Draft: board up 6", board down 2'3", Weight (loaded): 125 lbs., Cap.: 750 lbs., Sail Area: 44 s.f., Max. H.P.: 1.5

Approximate Price: Sailing model $1900.

O God, the strength of all those who put their trust in Thee, bless the company of this ship. Watch over us and keep us from all harm. With the power of Thy love deliver us from temptation that we may reach out home port with all the candles aflame on the altar of our souls. Consecrate with Thy presence, the way our feet should go that the way be made plain and the duty performed. Amen.

DOVER DORY 8'

The **DOVER DORY 8'** is constructed of hand laid fiberglass, with a wood insert to strengthen the transom for an outboard motor. She is built with bow and stern flotation tanks. This sailing dinghy is complete with one piece mast, boom, daggerboard, rudder, tiller, sail, sheets, blocks and trim.

The gunwales, thwarts, rudder, daggerboard and boom are hand crafted from solid mahogany, machine sanded and ready for sealer. Fasteners and hardware are stainless steel, and the mast is anodized aluminum. Sails for the **DOVER DORY** are available in a wide variety of colors. Add on options include an oar package, mahogany motor mount, rainbow or tanbark sail, sail window, boat cover, and much more.

Manufacturer: The PBJ Dory Company, 2024 Pacific Avenue, San Pedro, CA 90731. 213/519-8440

SPECIFICATIONS: DOVER DORY 8'
LOA: 8', Beam: 48", Weight: 75 lbs., Sail Area: 45 s.f.

Approximate Price: $995.

CLASSIC AND LA PLAYA 8'

This traditional lapstrake styled hull is hand-laid with gel coat interior and exterior surfaces with bow and stern flotation chambers. The transom has a solid mahogany insert for outboard motor and rudder strength.

The **CLASSIC** and **LA PLAYA** are solid, good looking dinghies and come complete with sail, running rigging, 2-piece aluminum mast, spruce boom, rudder, tiller, daggerboard and trim. All wood is sanded and sealed, ready for finish sanding, oil or varnish. A 2-color, blue and white, 3.8 ounce fully battened sail, full-cut for light wind performance, is standard equipment on all models of the **CLASSIC** and **LA PLAYA** . Both styles are also available in 7' and 10' models.

Your dinghy is probably the most used piece of gear on your yacht, doing double duty as transportation and entertainment. The folks from Classic Marine give you a fine traditional design, functional as well as fun...a dinghy that will suit your needs and give you pride.

The **CLASSIC** model comes with mahogany gunnels sandwiching the hull, through fastened for strength. The rudder, daggerboard and tiller are solid mahogany with stainless steel gudgeons and pintles. All blocks, pad-eyes and cleats are stainless for beauty and ease of maintenance. The standard rowing plug, as well as the daggerboard, fit flush to provide a smooth center seat.

The **LA PLAYA** model (shown in photo) is identical to the **Classic**, but also features solid teak trim, traditionally styled gunnels with recessed rope gunnel guard, slatted teak trim on the fore and aft seats and a flush daggerboard trunk for additional comfort when rowing. The **LA PLAYA** rigging features a halyard operated sail with one set of reef points and a topping lift to allow you to conveniently furl the sail on the boom. The hardware is upgraded to include brass oarlock sockets, brass tiller and gooseneck tangs, and cast brass gudgeons and pintles.

CLASSIC AND LA PLAYA 8'

For style, performance and value, look up Classic Marine Sailing Dinghies.

Manufacturer: Classic Marine, 2244 Main St., Ste. 3, Chula Vista, California 92011. 619/423-0206

SPECIFICATIONS: CLASSIC & LA PLAYA 8'
LOA: 8', LWL" 6'6", Beam: 47", Draft: board up - 4", board down - 2', Mast: 12', Sail Area: 45 s.f., Weight: 75 lbs.

Approximate Price: Classic - 7' $850, 8' $950, 10' $1050
La Playa - 7' $1250, 8' $1350, 10' $1550

PORTA-BOTE

    During the past few years, there has been a dramatic change in the lifestyles and values of outdoor enthusiasts. Many are now living in condominiums, apartments and smaller homes. They have little or no space to store ordinary craft. The incredible folding **PORTA-BOTE** stows easily in a closet or even under a bed.

    Many people are driving sub-compact automobiles, most of which are incapable of towing the larger, heavier boats. **PORTA-BOTE**, which is shaped like a surfboard when folded, neatly fits atop the smallest auto and ends trailering forever! RV'ers "hang" them on the side of their vehicles and owners of small sailboats and cabin

PORTA-BOTE

cruisers use the clever boats as ship to shore dinghies because they take up only 4" of valuable deck space.

These new craft are available in 8' (shown in photos), 10' and 12' models. They weigh in at an ultra-light 49, 59 and 69 lbs. respectively. Each sports a puncture proof polypropylene hull which carries a limited 10 year warranty. They can be easily opened or closed in less than 2 minutes; weigh half as much as comparable aluminum boats; cost less than the better inflatables; never need painting; are unaffected by salt water, fuel, even battery acid. And, according to the manufacturer, they're virtually unsinkable.

Manufacturer: Porta-Bote Int'l, 1074 Independence Avenue, Mountain View, CA 94043. 415/961-5334

SPECIFICATIONS: PORTA-BOTE 8'
LOA: 8', Beam: 58", Draft: 4", Weight 49 lbs. Capacity: 325 lbs. **Approximate Price:** $1300.

US SABOT

The **US SABOT** was originally the **Sidney Sabot**, manufactured by Lahaina Boats, prior to Capri Sailboats purchasing and improving the molds.

This is an excellent first boat for the beginning sailor, and a challenge for the experienced. The latest production methods make the **US SABOT** ultra-stiff, guaranteeing performance and durability, yet make it light enough to be car-topped and hand carried to the beach.

The simple rigging on the **US SABOT** allows one to experience the fundamentals of sailing.

Class Association: US Sabot Class Association, Kyle Stonecipher, 844 St. Charles Drive - #1, Thousand Oaks, CA 91360.

Manufacturer: Capri Sailboats, 21200 Victory Blvd., Woodland Hills, CA 91367. 818/884-7700

Manufacturer's Rep.: The Boat Works, 28710 Canwood St., #107, Agoura Hills, CA 91301. 818/991-0540

SPECIFICATIONS:
US SABOT
LOA: 8'
Beam: 46"
Weight: 68 lbs.
Sail Area: 38 s.f.

Approximate
Price: $990

US SABOT

DYER DHOW MIDGET

The **DYER DHOW MIDGET** is a most popular dinghy because it has proven to be the perfect size for most cruiser's auxiliaries. A rowing, sailing or "convertible" model is available.

The **MIDGET** also comes in a "Lo Sheer" model, specifically for deck house storage where boom clearance is a problem. It can be ordered with a translucent bottom, for use over a skylight.

DYER DHOW MIDGET

Like all **Dyer** dinghies, she is strong and light, is finished out beautifully and incorporates the very best materials for rigging and hardware. Every boat is hand-built. **Dyer** has been producing quality dinghies for over 50 years.

Manufacturer: The Anchorage, Inc. 57 Miller Street, Warren, Rhode Island 02885. 401/245-3300

SPECIFICATIONS: DYER DHOW MIDGET
LOA: 96.75", Beam: 49.25", Depth: 20", Draft: board up - 5.5", board down - 28.5", Hull Weight: 83 lbs., Capacity: 390 lbs.

SPECIFICATIONS: DYER DHOW MIDGET "LO SHEER"
LOA: 95.75", Beam: 46 7/8", Depth: 17", Draft: board up - 5.25", board down - 28.25", Hull Weight: 81 lbs., Capacity: 315 lbs.

Approximate Price: $1840.

For All Seafarers

"We pray to Thee, O God our heavenly Father, for all seafarers and for those who serve their needs: for the officers and men of the Navy and the Merchant Marine; for the keepers of light-houses and the pilots of our ports; for those who man lifeboats and guard our coasts; for the men of the fishing-fleets and those who carry out the services of docks and harbours; and for all guilds and societies which care for the well-being of sailors and their families. Bless them according to their several necessities, and keep them in all dangers and temptations. Through Jesus Christ our Lord. Amen."

PILOT DINGHY

PILOT DINGHIES were first produced in the early 70's in New England. The original manufacturer went out of business and the molds lay idle for several years. They have been back in production 5-6 years. Over 3000 of these popular dinghies have been sold.

The **PILOT DINGHY** comes in two sailing models, and four row/power models ranging from 7 feet to 9.5 feet.

The sailing models offered are the **8' CAPTAIN** (shown in photo) and the **9.5' ADMIRAL**. Both of these boats can be converted to row or power boats. The **ADMIRAL** model offers a sloop rig. All models have as standard equipment: oiled teak seats, bronze fittings, molded-in foam flotation, Dwyer standing rigging and anodized aluminum spars, and a unique rub rail that is guaranteed to last. Each boat also comes with a 4" inspection port for storing sunglasses, keys, etc.

These boats are built to last and offer many advantages as standard equipment. Of course, all boats can be rowed or powered with a 2 H.P. outboard.

A unique option offered by Starwing is that they will even mold your dinghy/tender to match your boat!

Manufacturer: Starwing, Inc., P.O. Box 137, Bristol, RI 02809. 401/254-0670

SPECIFICATIONS: PILOT DINGHY 8' CAPTAIN
LOA: 8'1", Beam: 50", Weight: 85 lbs., Sail Area: 42 s.f., Capacity: 475 lbs., Max. H.P.: 2

Approximate Price: $1099.

PILOT DINGHY

8' CAPTAIN

SAIL DINK

The eight foot **SAIL DINK** is a row/sail combination, designed to offer the added feature of a deluxe sail rig. The halyard controlled two piece mast can be removed in minutes to convert the **SAIL DINK** to a conventional eight foot boat that can be rowed or motored.

She is built of high quality hand laid fiberglass and has some unique features not found in other tenders her size. Her inner liner has a full gel coat and a center mahogany seat.

A six inch band of foam, 1.5 inches thick, provides gunnel flotation between the sides and inner liner, with additional foam flotation in the front and rear tanks.

The **SAIL DINK** utilizes a mahogany plywood daggerboard, rudder and centerboard trunk cover. Additional options include a davit ring kit, five foot wooden oars, round chrome oar lock horns and an acrylic boat cover.

Manufacturer:
American Sail, Inc.
7350 Pepperdam Ave.
Charleston, SC 29418
803/552-8548

SPECIFICATIONS:
SAIL DINK
LOA: 8'1"
Beam: 4'3"
Depth: 20"
Weight: 90 lbs.
Sail Area: 35 s.f.
Mast Height: 13'

Approximate
Price: $1150

SEA ROBIN

Compare her with far costlier sailing dinghies. The **SEA ROBIN** sails very well and can be rowed, towed or carried on davits. Her two-piece mast comes apart for in-boat storage. She carries Dacron sails, Nylon lines, stainless steel hardware, mahogany rudder, tiller and daggerboard.

Every Ensign Dinghy is built to the high quality standards of Mike Dapice, founder of Ensign Dinghies and Marine. Coremat construction assures strength as well as a lightweight hull. All hull fittings are backed by hardwood plates. Seats are molded in or solid mahogany. Interior and exterior is gelcoated for beauty as well as easy cleanup.

Manufacturer: Ensign Dinghies & Marine, Michael Dapice Enterprises, Inc., P.O. Box 547, Rye, NY 10580. 914/967-1656

SPECIFICATIONS:
SEA ROBIN
LOA: 8'1"
Beam: 3'10"
Depth: 19"
Sail Area: 42 s.f.
Weight: 80 lbs.
Capacity: 375 lbs.
Max. H.P.: 2

Approximate
Price: $800.

HOLDER HAWK

This sharp looking little dinghy by **Hobie Cat** is perfect for the young beginner. The youngsters will like it because she looks good, goes fast and is easy to sail. She offers optional oar locks and motor mount and can double as a yacht tender.

The **HOLDER HAWK** is unsinkable and can be righted easily, even by the light weight sailor. The cockpit is self-bailing, so upsets are quickly handled and you're on your way.

Every owner of a **HOLDER HAWK** is automatically a member of the class association. The program at **Hobie** includes newsletters and organized regattas. A portion of the money earned from each **HAWK** is donated by **Hobie Cat** to the United States Yacht Racing Union Junior Sailing Program.

Class Association: Holder Hawk Class Association, P.O. Box 1008, Oceanside, Ca 92054.

Manufacturer: Hobie Cat, P.O. Box 1008, Oceanside, CA 92054. 619/758-9100

SPECIFICATIONS:
HOLDER HAWK
LOA: 9'
LWL: 8'4"
Beam: 3'10.5"
Draft:
 board up 4.5"
 board down 2'3.5"
Hull Weight: 74 lbs.
Sail Area: 42 s.f.
Crew capacity: 1-2
Mast Height: 15'2"

Approximate Price: $1190.

HOLDER HAWK

NORDIC IX

Mike and Ruth Nilson have been producing dinghies since 1981. Their beautiful boat was awarded first prize in the 1986 Norwalk Oyster Festival small boat show.

The hull design of the **NORDIC** dinghy is the evolution of an old design originating from Northern European and Scandinavian waters. They were first used as shore boats for fishing vessels. However, their reputation for stability made them popular with pleasure boaters as well.

Every **NORDIC** is constructed of the finest materials available. The hull is hand laid-up with strength comparable to many 20-foot production boats. Full flotation chambers are bonded to the hull. Spars are all laminated spruce stained to match all the teak trim. All hardware is the very finest. This is a quality built dinghy.

She is finished off beautifully. Teak is the only wood used to finish trim. The entire hull interior is finished with gel-coat. The double gunwales are finished with three fourths inch nylon rope which provides an attractive, practical fender. The finish overall is elegant.

Her rowing characteristics are exceptional and feature half inch strait shank oarlock sockets and a pair of sockets in the center seat for storage when oars are not in use.

The sail on the **NORDIC** is a traditional gaff rig for simplicity and stability.

Manufacturer: Nordic Dinghy Company, 2635 175th Avenue N.E., Redmond, WA 98052. 206/881-2622

SPECIFICATIONS: NORDIC IX
LOA: 9', LWL: 8'2", Beam: 51", Draft: board down - 2'6", Weight: 145 lbs., Sail Area: 52 s.f.

Approximate Price: $1795.

DYER DHOW 9

The first **Dyer** dinghies were built of wood over 50 years ago. The **DYER DHOW 9**, like all **Dyer** dinghies, is built with quality craftsmanship, strength and beauty. There is no comparing this piece of work to other dinghies on the market. Her long life span, durability and ongoing pride of ownership far outlast dinghies in mass-production.

Today, the **DYER DHOW 9** is constructed of fiberglass, but still utilizes oak, mahogany and teak wherever there are advantages of strength, lightness and appearance.

The **DYER DHOW 9** is a reasonably expensive dinghy. But, her exceptional performance, quality materials and rigging, and superior longevity make her a very smart investment.

Manufacturer: The Anchorage, Inc., 57 Miller Street, Warren, Rhode Island 02885-0403. 401/245-3300

SPECIFICATIONS: DYER DHOW 9
LOA: 109 3/8"
Beam: 54 3/8"
Depth: 21 1/8"
Draft:
  board up 5.5"
  board down 33"
Hull Wt.: 104 lbs.
Capacity: 650 lbs.

Approximate Price: $1865

MK DINGHY

The **MK DINGHY** is the result of years of research creating an efficient, yet, sturdy yacht tender made up of a minimum of parts. An excellent small sailing dinghy for young and old, she also handles well with motors up to 4 horsepower, or under one or two pairs of oars.

The yacht tender was designed by the U.S. Navy under contract for 117 boats which were built as tenders for Air Force Crash boats. Later the Canadian Navy purchased the **MK DINGHY** as tenders for their new Arctic Icebreakers. Since this time, the **MK** has also be produced for other foreign countries and for another branch of our Armed Forces.

Standard equipment on the **MK** includes: air tanks (one forward and one aft) which are tested prior to delivery, mahogany pads for outboard motor, 2 sets of nylon rowlock sockets, one set of rowlocks complete with retainers, and vinyl rub rail.

The sailing model includes as additional equipment: rudder, tiller, centerboard, aluminum mast and boom, mast partners, main sheet halyard, and sail. For ease in storage, jointed spars are also available at extra charge.

This superb dinghy is used as a work boat, hauling heavy objects such as anchors or gear, etc. Boats of 5,000 lbs. are towed with comparative ease by the **MK**. Under daily use and sometimes abuse, it continues to be by far one of the best possible tenders.

Manufacturer: Cape Cod Shipbuilding, Wareham, MA 02571. 617/295-3550

SPECS: MK DINGHY
LOA: 9'1.5", Beam: 4'0", Depth: 1'6", Rowing Wt: 98 lbs., Sailing Wt: 125 lbs., Sail Area: 45 s.f.
Approximate Price: $1180

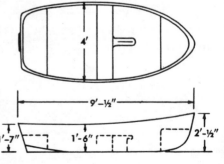

CAPTAIN'S LADY

A proud classical beauty for those with a discriminating eye for beauty and aesthetics - **CAPTAIN'S LADY**.

The **LADY** has a wine glass stern, deep skeg for rowing and towing. The lapstrake hull adds beauty and strength to her lines. Rubrails, center seat, rudder tiller and motor mounts are teak, finished with four coats of tung oil.

CAPTAIN'S LADY

The **LADY** carries Dacron sail, Nylon lines, anodized spars filled with foam flotation. All hardware is stainless steel or bronze. She is made of fiberglass and constructed of Coremat, which is strong and lightweight, and is a flotation material used in boats up to forty feet in length. In short, the **LADY** is a Lady.

Every Ensign Dinghy is built to the high quality standards of Mike Dapice, founder of Ensign Dinghies and Marine. All hull fittings are backed by hardwood plates. Seats are molded in or solid mahogany. Interior and exterior is gelcoated for beauty as well as easy cleanup.

Manufacturer: Ensign Dinghies & Marine, Michael Dapice Enterprises, Inc., P.O. Box 547, Rye, NY 10580. 914/967-1656

SPECIFICATIONS: CAPTAIN'S LADY
LOA: 9'6", Beam: 3'7", Depth: 1'7", Sail Area: 36 s.f., Weight: 75 lbs., Capacity: 375 lbs., Max. H.P.: 2

Approximate Price: $1300.

On Embarkation

Almighty God, we turn our thoughts to Thee as we make ready to sail for distant places. Thou knowest the future and will defend us from all adversities both to the soul and body if we will fully trust in Thee. Enable each of us to cheerfully accept his respective place of duty within this ship that we may pass all our days in devotion to our sacred tasks. Watch over our wives, children, and loved ones at home through all the days of our separation, that our return may be a blessed homecoming. Grant us a good ship's spirit, a happy voyage, and a safe return. Amen.

SEA HAWK

This beautiful classic design is the first choice of knowledgeable boatsmen who want the highest pointing, most responsive sailing dinghy available. With just 42 square feet of sail, the **SEA HAWK** out-runs dinghies that have 50% more sail. A fine frost bite dinghy, she has Dacron sails, two-piece anodized aluminum mast stainless steel hardware, mahogany rudder and daggerboard, oak tiller and nylon lines.

Every Ensign Dinghy is built to the high quality standards of Mike Dapice, founder of Ensign Dinghies and Marine. Coremat construction assures strength as well as a lightweight hull. All hull fittings are backed by hardwood plates. Seats are molded in or solid mahogany. Interior and exterior is gelcoated for beauty as well as easy cleanup.

Manufacturer: Ensign Dinghies & Marine, Michael Dapice Enterprises, Inc., P.O. Box 547, Rye, NY 10580. 914/967-1656

SPECIFICATIONS:
SEA HAWK
LOA: 9'6"
Beam: 4'1"
Depth: 2'
Sail Area: 42 s.f.
Weight: 110 lbs.
Capacity: 375 lbs.
Max. H.P.: 2

**Approximate
Price:** $990

SHRIMP

This all purpose, unsinkable dinghy is ideal as a tender. Her versatility makes her a perfect companion on family cruises. She tows extremely well, thanks to the skeg and low towing eye. Youngsters often get bored on long cruises, and the **SHRIMP** can provide lots of excitement. The addition of a small outboard motor or a rowing kit transforms the **SHRIMP** into a fishing boat.

Weighing only 120 pounds, the **SHRIMP** can easily be car-topped. She comes complete with mast, boom, kick-up rudder, centerboard, rigging and bright orange and white sails, which allows parents to spot their *"Shrimps"* from far away.

Manufacturer: Vandestadt & McGruer Ltd., Yacht Designers & Builders, P.O. Box 7, Owen Sound, Ontario Canada N4K 5P1. 519/376-8548

SPECIFICATIONS:
SHRIMP
LOA: 9'7"
Beam: 4'10"
Draft:
  board up 6"
  board down 2'6"
Weight: 120 lbs.
Sail Area: 50 s.f.

Approximate
Price: $1250

Almighty and everloving God, we most heartily thank Thee for Thy rich mercy in providing for our daily needs. We are conscious of the kindly forces which tie us together with the cords of ship life. Help us always to be good shipmates. Amen.

PERRYWINKLE 10

Those of you who have seen the **Perrywinkle 8** will readily recognize this handsome 10-foot addition to the line -- **PERRYWINKLE 10**.

After marketing Bob Perry's original sailing/row dinghy, Perrywinkle, Inc. saw no reason to change anything but the size. The new model exhibits the same qualities of ease in rowing, sailing, towing, maneuverability, stability and high-quality workmanship.

PERRYWINKLE 10

PERRYWINKLE 10 is cat-rigged and loose-footed for ease of sailing. She is equipped with the finest quality rigging and sail. Also available in a rowing model, she can be purchased without the teak seatgrates and floorboards.

Built to carry up to 1000 pounds, **PERRYWINKLE 10** can handle a maximum two horsepower engine. She is also available with gunnel guard, motor mount and drain plugs. Standard with the **PERRYWINKLE 10** is your choice of white or grey hull, but for a little extra money, you can get any color hull and striping you want.

If you're in the market for a dinghy, don't buy until you check out **PERRYWINKLE!**

Manufacturer: Perrywinkle, Inc., Annapolis City Marina, Suite 303, Annapolis, MD 21403. 301/269-0887

Manufacturer: Luna Yachts, Ltd., Unit 20, 427 Speers Road, Oakville, Ontario, Canada L6K 3S8. 416/842-4808

SPECIFICATIONS: PERRYWINKLE 10
LOA: 9'11", LWL 8'8", Beam: 5, Draft: board up 6", board down 2'5", Sail Area: 60 s.f., Capacity: 1000 lbs., Max. H.P.: 2

Approximate Price: Sailing model $2400

For Those Who Have Received Tragic News

Our Father, we ask Thee to encourage any of our shipmates who may have received tragic news from home. Cause them to continue with their best and leave all the doubtful outcomes in Thy merciful care. In the hours of the blackest night may they keep aflame the candle of faith that they may find their way toward their best possible solution. Amen

DYER DINK

Like all **Dyer** dinghies, the **DYER DINK** is an example of fine workmanship. A **Dyer** dinghy will last longer and perform better because it is hand-built. These dinghies are light but, at the same time, unusually strong and durable.

Quality materials in rigging and hardware put her far ahead of other dinghies on the market today. The first **Dyer** dinghies were built over 50 years ago, using wood. Fiberglass is used today, along with mahogany, oak

DYER DINK

and teak wherever there are advantages of strength, appearance and lightness.

Using careful control during the construction process, this dinghy is produced to stand up beautifully under heavy use.

The price of a **DYER DINK** is somewhat more than other dinghies you may find, but her superior craftsmanship, life span and durability make her worth the difference.

Manufacturer: The Anchorage, Inc., 57 Miller Street, Warren, Rhode Island 02885-0403. 401/245-3300

SPECIFICATIONS:
DYER DINK
LOA: 119 3/4"
Beam: 54 1/2"
Depth: 22 1/4"
Draft:
   board up 5.5"
   board down 46.5"
Hull Weight: 125 lbs.
Capacity: 740 lbs.

Approximate Price:
$2950.

O God of another day, look with favor upon our service in this ship. Grant us strength of body, mind, and spirit to render our best for Thee and our native land. Rebuke us when we offer our second best and forgive us when we become entangled in petty bickerings. Make us big men in all our dealings. Amen.

DOVER DORY 10'

The **DOVER DORY 10'** is constructed of hand laid fiberglass, with a wood insert to strengthen the transom for an outboard motor. She is built with bow and stern flotation tanks. This sailing dinghy is complete with one piece mast, boom, daggerboard, rudder, tiller, sail, sheets, blocks and trim.

The gunwales, thwarts, rudder, daggerboard and boom are hand crafted from solid mahogany, machine sanded and ready for sealer. Fasteners and hardware are stainless steel, and the mast is anodized aluminum. Sails for the **DOVER DORY** are available in a wide variety of colors. Add on options include an oar package, mahogany motor mount, rainbow or tanbark sail, sail window, boat cover, and much more.

Manufacturer: The PBJ Dory Company, 2024 Pacific Avenue, San Pedro, CA 90731. 213/519-8440

SPECIFICATIONS:
DOVER DORY 10'
LOA: 10'
Beam: 48"
Weight: 90 lbs.
Sail Area: 55 s.f.

Approximate
Price: $1095.

TRINKA

The **TRINKA** dinghy was designed by Bruce P. Bingham, N.A. in 1972. Her gracefully curved, slightly "wineglass" transom and plumb bow give her a classic and distinctive air. The **TRINKA**, available in 8' and 10' (shown in photo), stands out with a most ladylike personality.

She was conceived not to cut production expenses nor to compete in the market, but to be rugged, practical and reliable. Hundreds of "one-off" **TRINKA**s have been produced around the world. To assure the most faithful reproduction, Mr. Bingham supervised the hull lofting, oversaw the plug and mold development and created dozens of special assembly drawings for the builder.

The **TRINKA** has proven itself over the years. It is the only fiberglass dinghy endorsed by critical author and famous world sailor, Donald M. Street. This dinghy was featured in the *The Complete Live-Aboard Book* by K. M. Burke. Jeff Spranger, editor of *The Practical Sailor*, says, "I couldn't find a really good dinghy, so I had to build my own" (Jeff's dinghy is a **Trinka**.)

Mr. Bingham's own **TRINKA** has been in use for more than ten years. It has withstood thousands of miles of towing, has taxied millions of pounds and has been kissed by a thousand beaches. The **TRINKA** is definitely a standard-setter.

Manufacturer: Johannsen Boat Works, P.O. Box 570097, Miami, FL 33257-0097. 305/445-7534

SPECIFICATIONS:
TRINKA 10
LOA: 10'
Beam: 50"
Weight: 125 lbs.
Height: 28"

Approximate Price:
Sail $2400, Row $1650

TRINKA

TRINKA 10

SWEET SUE

She's a classical, large capacity dinghy with a lapstrake hull that adds beauty and strength. All wood parts are teak, finished with four coats of tung oil -- rubrails, center seat, rudder, tiller and motor mount. SWEET SUE has Dacron sail, Nylon lines and anodized spars filled with foam flotation. All hardware is stainless steel or bronze. She is made of fiberglass and Coremat, a strong, lightweight flotation material.

Every Ensign Dinghy is built to the high quality standards of Mike Dapice, founder of Ensign Dinghies and Marine. Coremat construction assures strength as well as a lightweight hull. All hull fittings are backed by hardwood plates. Seats are molded in or solid mahogany. Interior and exterior is gelcoated for beauty as well as easy cleanup.

Manufacturer: Ensign Dinghies & Marine, Michael Dapice Enterprises, Inc., P.O. Box 547, Rye, NY 10580. 914/967-1656

SPECIFICATIONS:
SWEET SUE
LOA: 10'
Beam: 4'3"
Depth: 24"
Sail Area:
 Main 42 s.f.
 Jib 20 s.f.
Weight: 125 lbs.
Capacity: 450 lbs.
Max.H.P.:4

Approximate Price: $1500.

WHITEHALL 10

You'll find the **WHITEHALL 10** is designed to be a versatile tender, long enough to row well, yet light enough to handle easily. She's available with a traditional sprit sail, which is fast to rig and stowable inside the boat.

Taken from traditional **WHITEHALL** lines, she is stable, light weight, easily handled by one person, and can be car-topped.

Top quality materials, such as varnished mahogany seats and gunnels, bronze hardware and hand laid up fiberglass, are the mark of all **B&S WHITEHALLS**.

Manufacturer: B&S Corp., Harrison C. Sylvester, Bessey Ridge Road, Albion, Maine 04910. 207/437-9245

SPECIFICATIONS:
WHITEHALL 10
LOA: 10'
Beam: 48"
Weight: 100 lbs.
Sail Area: 44 s.f.

Approximate
Price:
Row - $945
Sail - $1445

BAUER 10

The **BAUER 10** was designed by Hans- Christof Bauer as the ideal yacht tender for the serious cruiser. This beautiful dinghy was first introduced to the general public at the 1986 Miami Boat Show and is gaining popularity rapidly -- even as a great little daysailer.

Her displacement hull design, wide beam, high freeboard and unique layout ensure stability and high performance, even under adverse conditions or when fully loaded. The **BAUER 10** has a superbly finished interior design. Her unique forward and aft seats provide ample seating and double as storage compartments, with positive flotation available upon request.

Not only an exceptional sailboat, she is also a very functional rowboat. Her generous beam, high freeboard and sharp bow keep the boat stable and dry when rowing or when under power, and also reduce drag to a minimum when being towed.

BAUER 10

The **BAUER 10** will amaze you with her versatility and ease of handling under sail. The Gunter rigged reefable mainsail and jib provide excellent maneuvering ability and allow her to tack to windward with ease. The fiberglass rudder and centerboard kick up automatically when you beach the boat.

Manufacturer: Bauteck Marine Corp., Inc., 88 South Dixie Highway, St. Augustine, Florida 32084. 904/824-8826

SPECIFICATIONS:
BAUER 10
LOA: 10'1", Beam: 4'9", Draft: board up - 4", board down - 24", Sail Area: 53 s.f., Weight: 120 lbs.

Approximate Price: $1650.

TERN

Unlike most dinghies built today which are mass produced economy models, often with short life spans, each **TERN** is hand-built by N.L. Silva and his assistant. Careful attention is given the building process to produce

a boat that stands up to heavy use. These dinghies perform whether you sail, row, tow or power with a small outboard.

TERN

The **TERN** is widely used as a yacht tender, daysailer, junior trainer, or recreational rowing boat. Her large capacity and size make her a very versatile dinghy. Available in a sailing or rowing version, she is an exciting daysailer and her Whitehall heritage makes her an excellent rowing boat, as every tender should be.

She is finished beautifully, including such touches as mahogany trim, bronze oarlocks and socket, laminated spruce spars and rope fender. Mr. Silva also offers this fine craft in the 8' **Teal** and 12' **Gull** models, as well.

Manufacturer: N.L. Silva & Co., 7980 Market St., Wilmington, NC 28405. 919/686-4356

SPECIFICATIONS: TERN
LOA: 10'1", Beam: 4', Draft: board up - 3", board down - 24", Sail Area: 47 s.f., Weight: 100 lbs., Capacity: 500 lbs.

Approximate Price: $1600.

A Wartime Prayer

O God, our help in ages past, our hope today and tomorrow, we approach Thee in deep humility at this hour of tragic crisis. Forgive us, if we have contributed to the cause of this war in which Thy children are engaged. Protect the women, the children and the innocent. So fill our hearts with trust in Thee, that in peace and war we may commit our loved ones and ourselves to Thy never-failing care. Let not the powers of the darkness and of terror keep us from doing our duty as free men. Help us to fight on till all strife and oppression cease and the peoples of the world be delivered from bondage and fear. Give us victory, O God, if it be Thy will, but above all give us the knowledge that we are fighting for values that are right and everlasting. Amen.

THE TEN

In an easy to sail size, **THE TEN** is successfully used in Junior Sailing Programs. But, it is also owned and sailed by sail makers and national sailing champions.

THE TEN is a one-design class, featuring standard sail-away items not offered by many manufacturers. Some of those features are: hand-laid fiberglass construction, Dacron sail and battens, internal positive flotation, hiking strap, vang and outhaul, drain plug and much more.

She also can be equipped with an optional "Race Pack" including: all Harken blocks, 5 to 1 main sheet with cam cleat, 4 to 1 outhaul split port and starboard, 2 to 1 cunningham eye-split port and starboard, 2 to 1 boom vang with cam cleat, 5/8" anodized aluminum hiking stick, kick-up rudder, self bailing cockpit, and bow cleat. For a slight extra charge, **THE TEN** can be purchased with multi-color sails, hull and nonskid color.

THE TEN - She's ideal for beginners, yet provides excitement for the pros!

Class Association: The Ten Class Association 124 South Main Street, Andover, Ohio 44003.

Manufacturer: J. Melton Sailboats, Inc., 124 S. Main Street, Andover, Ohio 44003. 216/293-5822

SPECIFICATIONS:
THE TEN
LOA: 10'3"
Beam: 45"
Sail Area: 75 s.f.
Hull Weight: 85 lbs.
Racing Crew: 1
Capacity: 2

Approximate
Price: $1875

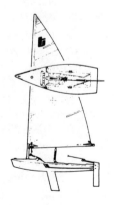

THE TEN

MIRROR

The **MIRROR** dinghy was designed in 1962 by Jack Holt after a British newspaper, *The Daily Mirror*, asked him to team up with Barry Bucknell, a TV handyman, to produce a dinghy that would provide the opportunity to sail to almost anyone. Their specifications were tough. She had to be a kit that could be built by a teenager, small and light enough to carry/cartop, yet provide good quality sailing for both family daysailing or racing. She also had to have a price lower than other boats on the market.

Barry developed the building method that was simple, yet sturdy and safe. Jack then designed this beautiful dinghy around the construction method.

The **MIRROR** dinghy has become one of the most famous in the world. There are over 70,000 world-wide. This little sloop-rig can be sailed cat-rigged or with jib and spinnaker because of the two-position mast. She rows well and will take a small outboard. The rigging is

MIRROR

simple, yet very efficient. This is one of the finest designs ever produced and you can build it yourself from a kit or purchase ready to sail.

Class Association: U.S. Mirror Class Assn., John Borthwick, Secretary, 5305 Marian Drive, Lyndhurst, Ohio 44124.

Manufacturer: Mirror Sailcraft of Canada, RR #1, Redbridge, Ontario, Canada, P0H 2A0. 705/663-2751

SPECIFICATIONS:
MIRROR
LOA: 10'10"
Beam: 4'7"
Draft:
  board up 6"
  board down 2'6"
Weight: 135 lbs.
Sail Area: 69 s.f.

Approximate
Price
Ready-to-Sail: $2450
Complete Kit: $1350

An Easter Prayer

O Thou Son of God and Son of Man, who by Thy victory didst conquer the grave, raise us up from despair and loss of hope and deliver us from the darkness of unbelief and doubt. Set our affections upon the things above that we may have a good effect upon the activity of this ship. On this day we pause to render our praise for life's resurrections. For new hopes and new opportunities, we give Thee thanks. Send Thy spirit into our hearts. Amen.

DINGHIES AND DAYSAILERS /

11' To 13.99'

INTERNATIONAL MOTH CLASS

The **INTERNATIONAL MOTH** evolved from two separate events from opposite sides of the globe. In 1928, Len Morris designed and built an 11 foot cat-rigged scow that became popular as the **"Inverloch Class"** in Australia. At approximately the same period, around Atlantic City,

Capt. Joel Van Sant also designed and built and 11 foot cat-rigged dinghy for off-duty dinghy rowing with other ship's sailors while in port. Van Sant called his class the **MOTH**. In 1933, Len Morris requested the International

INTERNATIONAL MOTH CLASS

Moth Class Association for permission to use the name **MOTH** for his craft. Permission was granted the Inverloch Class to make the change. In 1970, 17 national associations became one under the sponsorship of the International Yacht Racing Union of London, England and formed the International Moth Class (World).

This is strictly a developmental class which encourages members to use their skill and imagination in developing new designs, methods of construction, materials, etc. to make faster, stronger, and lighter boats. Almost anything goes, as long as the hull is no longer than 11 feet and no wider than 7'4". The class association has plans available. Most boats are home-made and these do-it-yourselfers have produced many classy racing hulls.

There are 17 associations world-wide presently. This is a great class for the sailor who enjoys the thrill of sailing a light, hot boat like the **Laser**, but wants to build it himself and be able to experiment with his boat and at very low costs.

Class Association: International Moth Class Association, Benjamin Krothe III, 705 South Shore Road, Palermo, NJ 08223.

SPECIFICATIONS:
MOTH
LOA: 11'
Beam:
 less than 7'4"
Sail area: 85 s.f.

Approximate
Price: $800-1200
(do-it-yourself).

NORDIC XI

Mike and Ruth Nilson have been producing dinghies since 1981. Their beautiful boat was awarded first prize in the 1986 Norwalk Oyster Festival small boat show.

The hull design of the **NORDIC** dinghy is the evolution of an old design originating from Northern European and Scandinavian waters. They were first used as shore boats for fishing vessels. However, their reputation for stability made them popular with pleasure boaters as well.

NORDIC XI

Every **NORDIC** is constructed of the finest materials available. The hull is hand laid-up with strength comparable to many 20-foot production boats. Full flotation chambers are bonded to the hull. Spars are all laminated spruce, stained to match all the teak trim. All hardware is the very finest. This is a quality built dinghy.

She is finished off beautifully. Teak is the only wood used to finish trim. The entire hull interior is finished with gel-coat. The double gunwales are finished with three fourths inch nylon rope which provides an attractive, practical fender. The finish overall is elegant.

Her rowing characteristics are exceptional and feature half inch straight shank oarlock sockets and a pair of sockets in the center seat for storage when oars are not in use.

The sail on the **NORDIC** is a traditional gaff rig for simplicity and stability. Also featured on the **NORDIC XI** is a removable bow sprit and jib.

Manufacturer: Nordic Dinghy Company, 2635 175th Avenue N.E., Redmond, WA 98052. 206/881-2622

SPECIFICATIONS: NORDIC XI
LOA: 11' (12'10" with bowsprit), LWL: 9'10", Beam: 54", Draft: board down - 3', Weight: 200 lbs., Sail Area: 72 s.f. (96 s.f. with jib).

Approximate Price: $2095.

Almighty God, Father of mercies and sustainer of all those who are in sorrow, we pray for our shipmates who bear heavy burdens. May they heed Thy invitation "Come unto me all ye that labor and are heavy laden." May our claim be grounded in Thee and all our choices be governed by Thy will. Amen.

SUNDANCER & SUNFLOWER

These fine ultra-lights are similar in many ways to the **Super Snark**. They have a wider beam and a little stronger hull, allowing for additional sail area and more performance. These are also great smooth water starter boats, especially when hand-carrying is required or low price is a high priority.

The hull on both models is identical. Both are constructed of Armorclad™ surface molded over polystyrene. The **SUNFLOWER** carries a lateen rig, whereas, the **SUNDANCER** carries a cat-rig with added sail area for higher performance.

Simple, fun and fast -- both have room for two, are unsinkable and very simple to rig. The hull weighs only 50 pounds, so handling on shore is no problem.

Manufacturer: Snark Boats, P.O. Box 2360, Industrial St., New Castle, PA 16102. 412/658-6555

SPECIFICATIONS: SUNFLOWER & SUNDANCER
LOA: 11', Beam: 42", Sail Area: **Sunflower** 60 s.f., **Sundancer** 55 s.f., Capacity: 310 lbs., Hull Weight: 50 lbs.

Approximate Price: Sundancer $649, Sunflower $599.

Sundancer

Sunflower

Sundancer (left) & Sunflower

SUPER SNARK & SEA SNARK

SUPER SNARK is the old, famous polystyrene **SEA SNARK** with a tough cladding applied over the foam, called Armorclad™. This cladding protects the foam and makes the boat much more durable. The original **SEA SNARK** is still available after over 20 years of production.

Thousands of people have learned to sail in a **SNARK**, probably because it is one of the easiest to sail, and the cost is low. I personally observed one **SNARK** that handled the abuse of at least ten young sailors for several summers on a beach in Wakasa Wada, Japan. My son and daughter were part of the group, and both learned to sail in that **SNARK**. I was amazed at the durability of that little polystyrene boat. The kids would race me in my catamaran and, in light air, would win.

At only 50 pounds, the **SUPER SNARK** (30 pounds for the **SEA SNARK**) and the simple lateen rig, this is a great boat for the kids. But you won't be able to keep the adults out of it either.

Manufacturer: Snark Boats, P.O. Box 2360, Industrial St., New Castle, PA 16102. 412/658-6555

SPECIFICATIONS: SUPER SNARK & SEA SNARK
LOA: 11', Beam: 38", Sail Area: 45 s.f., Capacity: 2, Hull Weight: Super Snark - 50 lbs., Sea Snark - 30 lbs.
Approximate Price: Super Snark $549, Sea Snark $395.

Super Snark

Sea Snark

SUPER SNARK & SEA SNARK

SUPER SNARK

GLOUCESTER 11

The **GLOUCESTER 11** is an extremely versatile sailing and general purpose dinghy. Primarily a family boat, her deep, roomy cockpit can accommodate an average family of four safely and comfortably. This design feature permits a family to get by with the purchase of just a single boat, suitable for a variety of purposes, such as sailing, fishing, rowing and motoring.

An excellent boat for beginners, her cockpit is completely self-bailing, both underway and at rest. The buoyancy under the seats and foredeck and her foam flotation enable her to be rescued by her crew without assistance, even if swamped. Being extra dry, she makes an excellent boat for frostbite sailing, college racing and for junior sailing programs.

With her molded-in skeg giving her good directional stability, the **GLOUCESTER 11** makes a fine, roomy rowboat or yacht tender, capable of carrying up to four adults. Equipped with a small outboard, she becomes an all-purpose dinghy, suitable for fishing or crabbing. The transom is specially reinforced to carry outboard without a special bracket.

Light enough to cartop, easy to trailer, she can be launched, hauled and rigged by one person in minutes.

Manufacturer: Gloucester Yachts, Inc., P.O. Box 307, Route 623, Gloucester, Virginia 23061. 804/693-3818

SPECIFICATIONS: GLOUCESTER 11
LOA: 11'1", LWL: 10'3", Beam: 5'2", Draft: Hull 3", board down 2'9", Sail Area: 88 s.f., Mast Length: 18', Mast Clearance: 19'8", Weight: Hull 150 lbs., Rigged 200 lbs.

Approximate Price: $2200

GLOUCESTER 11

SKUNK & SUPER SKUNK

This rugged dinghy has been the choice of over a thousand owners. The main reason for the SKUNK's success is her versatility.

Under sail, she performs smoothly and can handle extremely rough conditions. The reinforced transom can take a small outboard motor or when combined with the optional rowing kit, the SKUNK becomes an ideal fishing boat. She is unsinkable, and the gaff rig is easy to set up and stows inside the boat. There is ample stowage under the fore deck.

The success of this boat led to the recent introduction of the SUPER SKUNK. She is the same multipurpose design, but for added sailing performance, the rig has been modified to be a stayed sloop rig. There is 25% more sail area, some extra blocks and cleats, and lots more sailing thrill!

Manufacturer: Vandestadt & McGruer Ltd., Yacht Designers & Builders, P.O. Box 7, Owen Sound, Ontario Canada, N4K 5P1. 519/376-8548

SPECIFICATIONS: SKUNK & SUPER SKUNK
LOA: 11'1", Beam: 5'5", Draft: centerboard up - 6", centerboard down - 2'6", Weight: 190 lbs., Sail Area: Skunk 70 s.f., Super Skunk 88 s.f.
Approximate Price: Skunk - $1575.   Super Skunk - $1875.

Skunk

Super Skunk

CL 11

Rugged, durable and an excellent choice for beginners, the **CL 11** may also be fitted with oarlocks for rowing. She is ideal for teaching children to sail, as she has a double-chined hull, wide beam and simple sloop rig.

The **CL 11** now has a larger jib than she used to. And, hiking strap, tiller extension and boweye are now standard equipment. She is easily taken to the water and her mast-stepping is pure simplicity: only one turnbuckle to adjust.

Convenient for launching and beaching are her pivoting mahogany centerboard and rudder blade -- also great for sailing where the water is shallow.

Manufacturer: C & L Boatworks, 884 Dillingham Road, Pickering, Ontario, Canada L1W 1Z6. 416/839-7991

SPECIFICATIONS: CL 11
LOA: 11'3", LWL: 10', Beam: 4'10", Sail Area: 86 s.f., Draft: centerboard up - 8", centerboard down - 3', Weight: 170 lbs.

Approximate Price: $2350 (Canadian Currency).

PENGUIN

The **PENGUIN** was developed around 1938 after a small group of Potomac and Chesapeake Bay area sailors wrote to leading naval architects for a small dinghy design that could be easily built at home by an amateur. Phillip Rhodes answered with a boat that could be built of plywood. Many **PENGUINS** are still home built. However, they can be purchased in wood or fiberglass today.

The **PENGUIN** Class Association actually began after *Yachting Magazine* printed an article with plans on the **PENGUIN** in 1940 which resulted in an overwhelming response requesting plans. This strict one-design class quickly grew to 7400 boats registered in 150 fleets. The **PENGUIN** participates in national and international racing for both adults and juniors.

PENGUIN

The **PENGUIN** is a good choice for anyone interested in dinghy racing, or just a good small dinghy for daysailing that can be built at home, or purchased. Many, if not most, are used in "frostbiting" fleets today.

Class Association: Penguin Class Association, Steven Shepstone, 26 Sheppard Street, Glen Head, NY 11545.

Manufacturer: Exact Boat Company Inc., Andrew K. Menkart 2827 Buren Avenue, Camden, NJ 08105. 609/541-4600

Manufacturer: Freedom Boatworks, Tony Bries, P.O. Box 511, Baraboo, WI 53913. 608/356-5861

SPECIFICATIONS:
PENGUIN
LOA: 11'5"
LWL: 11'3"
Beam: 4'8"
Hull Wt: 140 lbs.
Sail Area: 72 s.f.

Approximate
Price: $3600.

O God, save us from deserting ourselves like a crew leaving a ship abandoned to drift with no power to move and no port to make. Take the wheel and save us from being pilotless. We have Thy word as our chart. Fill our lives with Thy spirit that we may sail distant waters to see the wonders of the Lord in the deep. Amen.

MISTRAL FUN

Revolutionary in the sailing world! Mistral, with numerous years of pleasure craft manufacturing, perfected a totally new concept of sailing. The **MISTRAL FUN**, new and exciting, is perfect for the sport-minded enthusiast who wishes to discover a new trend in sailing.

The **FUN** is perfectly steamlined, well balanced, fast and responsive to the slightest command. She obtains maximum performance of light air and cuts through the wave with ease. She is a versatile sailboat which offers pleasure, stability, safety and performance. **MISTRAL FUN** is easily car-topped and is the answer to the dreams and aspirations of many sailing enthusiasts.

Manufacturer: Canadian Yacht Builders, P.O. Box 67, Dorion, Quebec, Canada J7V 5V8. 514/455-6183

SPECIFICATIONS: MISTRAL FUN
LOA: 11'6", LWL: 11', Beam: 4'2", Draft: board up 1', board down 2'6", Weight: 95 lbs., Sail Area: Novice 60 s.f., Intermediate 70 s.f., Expert 80 s.f.   **Approx. Price:** $1325.

INTERCLUB

The **INTERCLUB** dinghy is probably most famous as the class used in the popular "Frostbiting" regattas in the northeast. These regattas have been going on for over fifty years.

She was designed in 1946 by Sparkman and Stephens as a club boat for the Leachmont Yacht Club in New York. The original **INTERCLUB** was made of wood, but in the late 1950's, George O'Day began building her in fiberglass.

The **INTERCLUB** is a basic dinghy. She carries main only and does not plane. She is not usually equipped with any go-fast gear, yet she draws many famous sailors year after year.

There are eight organized fleets in existence. All are in the New England and New York areas. Association rules specify a boat weight of 250 lbs. (min.) and a crew of two with at least 315 pounds combined weight.

This is an amazing class. The boat appears to be simple, slow and overloaded (two adults in an eleven and a half foot dinghy). Yet, every year many champion one-design sailors (and every other kind of sailor) bundle up and brave the freezing temperatures to sail this little dinghy in one of the most competitive classes in the country. Is it the boat? Is it the people? Who knows, but it certainly is exciting!

Class Association: National Interclub Frostbite Dinghy Association, Marianne Borowski, Class President, 437 Marlborough St., Boston, MA 02115.

Manufacturer: Exact Boat Co., Inc., 2827 Buren Avenue, Camden, NJ 08105. 609/541-6800

SPECIFICATIONS: INTERCLUB
LOA: 11'6", Beam: 4' 7.5", Draft: 3'11", Weight: 250 lbs.

Approximate Price: $3000.

90

INTERCLUB

Photo by: David C. LaChapelle

SAILING SKIFF 12

This 12' Whitehall skiff is an exciting sailer that really gets up and goes in a stiff breeze and also performs responsively in light airs. The sail can be reefed as wind conditions dictate. The spritsail rig stows in the boat and can be set up in minutes.

As a rowing boat, the **SAILING SKIFF 12** tracks beautifully, yet maneuvers easily at the command of the oars. This hull shape handles less than ideal sea conditions very well.

SAILING SKIFF 12

This skiff is a dry, genteel, multi-use water craft. You can sail, row, motor, fish, camp tour, or use it as a tender to a larger boat. Two adults can be carried sailing or three rowing.

She's constructed of epoxy encapsulated mahogany, finished clear on the inside and the exterior of the wineglass transom; white on the outside with linear polyurethane finishes.

Manufacturer: Bad River Boatworks, James M. Taber, Boatbuilder, Box 98, Brant, MI 48614. 517/585-3514

SPECIFICATIONS: SAILING SKIFF 12
LOA: 11'9", Beam: 3'11", Weight: 115 lbs., Sail Area: 44 s.f. Max. H.P.: 3.

Approximate Price: $4850

ECHO

Designed for today's recreational market, the **ECHO** is a fast and safe boat. She is light and easy to handle ashore and afloat. This boat can be rigged and ready to sail in minutes, yet has all the equipment necessary to sail as a modern high performance dinghy.

The **ECHO** was developed as a family sailboat, and careful attention to detail allowed the designer to incorporate many features into the boat. Her fiberglass hull and deck form natural flotation tanks. In addition, positive foam buoyancy adds to the boat safety. The cockpit has plenty of room for four people, and the rudder kicks up to allow easy sailing near the beach.

A large storage compartment is provided under the foredeck to allow for gear and accessories. All fittings and lines are made from high quality marine materials. The **ECHO** is easily driven under sail and can also be used for rowing and motoring.

Manufacturer: C & L Boatworks, 884 Dillingham Road, Pickering, Ontario, Canada L1W 1Z6.

SPECIFICATIONS:
ECHO
LOA: 11'10"
Beam: 4'11"
Draft:
 board up 4"
 board down 24"
Hull Wt.: 140 lbs.
Sail Area: 92 s.f.

Approximate
Price: $2560
(Canadian Currency)

ECHO

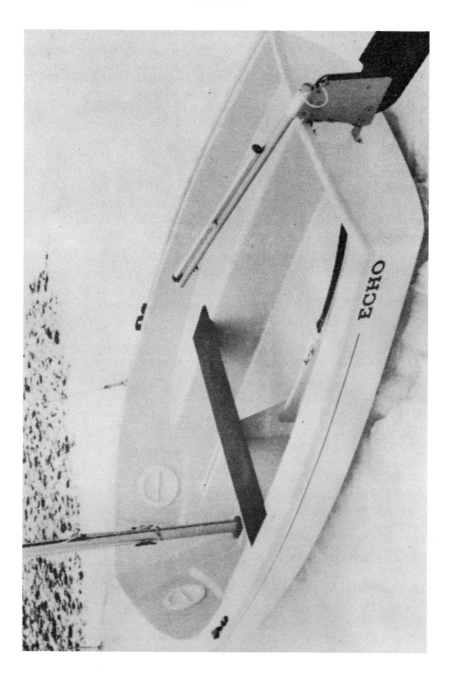

JOHNSON MINI-SCOW

According to Johnson Boat Works, their **MINI-SCOW** is *"simply the best 12 foot sailboat ever built."*

They took the best features of many small sailboats, plus some great ideas of their own, and combined them to build a great boat. She is extremely roomy and comfortable, easy to rig, and easy to sail.

The **MINI-SCOW**'s free-standing spar with a halyard hoist sail makes rigging a breeze. The attention to detail is unequaled, from the padded hiking straps, to the white vinyl protective hull molding and Harken cams. Whether you're a first time sailor or an old salt, you'll agree, the Johnson **MINI-SCOW** is simply one of the best!

Manufacturer:
Johnson Boat Works,
4495 Lake Avenue,
White Bear Lake,
MN 55110.
612/429-7221

SPECIFICATIONS:
JOHNSON
MINI-SCOW
LOA: 12'
Beam: 54"
Draft:
 board up 2"
 board down 26"
Weight: 140 lbs.
Sail Area: 72 s.f.
Mast Length: 18'

Approximate
Price: $1695

TEAL

This sharp looking, simple plywood double-ender is offered by the famous builder Harold H. "Dynamite" Payson. The design is by Phil Bolger, who has designed many of the these plywood boats primarily for the home builder. You can purchase the **TEAL** from Harold ready to sail or you can build it in approximately 40 hours of spare time. Plans are $20.00.

Harold also has plans for about 20 other designs and offers a study packet of all for $3.00.

Manufacturer: Harold H. Payson, Pleasant Beach Road, South Thomaston, ME 04858. 207/594-7587

SPECIFICATIONS: TEAL
LOA: 12', Beam: 3'6", Weight: 93 lbs.

Approximate Price: $950.

HOLDER 12

The **HOLDER 12** was designed for lighter weight persons looking for high performance. This racy, good looking, simply rigged dinghy is ideal for folks weighing under 180 pounds, and a 90 pound youngster can handle her easily.

Her sleeved mainsail and cat-boat rig make for simple rigging and sailing. The mast breaks down into sections. With all this and a light 115 pound hull, she is a good boat for car-topping and launching where no ramps are available. The **HOLDER 12**'s flip-up rudder allows sailing right up on the beach.

She's unsinkable and easy to right after capsizing. The cockpit is self bailing.

Ownership of the this boat makes class membership automatic. **HOLDER** fleets organize regattas and family outings in many, many areas.

Class Association: Holder 12 Class Association, P.O. Box 1008, Oceanside, CA 92054.

Manufacturer: Hobie Cat, P.O. Box 1008, Oceanside, CA 92054. 619/758-9100

SPECIFICATIONS:
HOLDER 12
LOA: 12'
LWL: 11'3"
Beam: 5'
Draft:
 board up 6"
 board down 2'6"
Sail Area: 68 s.f.
Capacity: 350 lbs.
Mast Height: 18'

**Approximate
Price:** $1350.

HOLDER 12

SEA DEVIL & SUNCATCHER

This is an ultra light weight, fun, board-type daysailer. At only 55 pounds and 70 square feet of sail, the **SEA DEVIL** (shown in photo) is wet and wild. If the 70 square foot sloop rig is too much for you, the same hull comes with a 55 square foot lateen rig, called the **SUN CATCHER.**

These daysailers are ideal for the sailor who just wants to have fun with simplicity and low cost. You can carry these boats down to the water and be sailing in five minutes.

Manufacturer: Snark Boats, P. O. Box 2360, Industrial Street, New Castle, PA 16102. 412/658-6555

SPECIFICATIONS: SEA DEVIL & SUNCATCHER
LOA: 12', Beam: 39", Capacity: 475 lbs., (3 people), Weight: 55 lbs., Sail Area: Main - 55 s.f., Jib (Sea Devil) - 15 s.f.

Approximate Price: Sea Devil or Suncatcher $650.

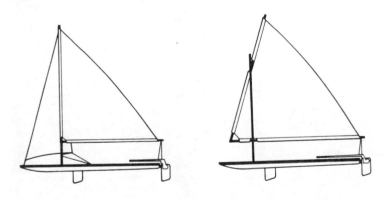

Sea Devil   Sun Catcher

SEA DEVIL & SUNCATCHER

SEA DEVIL

SUNCHASER

The 12' **SUNCHASER** is manufactured in two models. These are the largest in the **Snark** line.

With 72 s.f. of lateen rig, the **SUNCHASER I** converts to a rowboat with standard oar locks. She will also handle an outboard up to six horse power. These features make her simple and very versatile.

The **SUNCHASER II** is the most powerful boat made by Snark. With a sloop rig and a tall mast, the 100 s.f. of sail make this boat a real performer.

SUNCHASER I

Both boats have big lockable bow compartments for storage, which double as built-in coolers. They have

SUNCHASER

foam-filled hulls, making them unsinkable. Their light weight makes them ideal for car-topping and for situations where manually carrying the boats is required.

SUNCHASER II

Manufacturer: Snark Boats, P. O. Box 2360, Industrial Street, New Castle, PA 16102. 412/658-6555

SPECIFICATIONS: SUNCHASER I & SUNCHASER II
LOA: 12', Beam 56", Weight: 125 lbs., Capacity: 900 lbs., Sail Area: **Sunchaser I** - 72 s.f., **Sunchaser II** - Main: 80 s.f., Jib: 20 s.f.

Approx. Price: Sunchaser I - $1449, Sunchaser II - $1595.

THE TWELVE

This hot looking dinghy, designed by Jim Melton, appears to be a well made little boat. **THE TWELVE** is ideal for juniors and beginners, or anyone looking for an inexpensive, light-weight, small daysailer. The cockpit is roomy for this type of boat and can be sailed by two persons. Positive flotations, self bailing and easy righting make it a fun summer-time boat.

A two cubic foot storage locker provides space for your picnic, etc. There is also an optional "Race Pack" available, if you are interested in class or Portsmouth racing. It includes all Harken blocks, boom vang, 5 to 1 main sheet, kick-up rudder, and other go-fast gear.

THE TWELVE is fast, safe, easy to sail, and will cartop on the smallest compact car. Class rules provide quality of competition. **THE TWELVE** provides the maximum sailing enjoyment for minimum dollars.

Class Association: The Twelve Class Association 124 South Main Street, Andover, Ohio 44003.

Manufacturer: J. Melton Sailboats, Inc., 124 S. Main St., Andover, Ohio 44003. 216/293-5822

SPECIFICATIONS:
THE TWELVE
LOA: 12'
Beam: 48"
Sail Area: 75 s.f.
Hull Weight: 100 lbs.
Racing Crew: 1
Capacity: 2

Approximate
Price: $2000

THE TWELVE

WHITEHALL 12

"We found a 12-foot WHITEHALL at least 100 years old in a family boat house in Houlton and made a mold for the fiberglass from it. The original is now on display at the Bath Marine Museum", says Harry Sylvester, manufacturer of the **WHITEHALL**. This design dates back at least 300 years. It has evolved through centuries to become one of the most popular rowing boats. The name for this boat could have come from Whitehall Street in New Amsterdam (now New York City), where it was originally constructed.

The **WHITEHALL** 12' is the most popular of Sylvester's fleet, which includes 10, 16 and 22 footers. The 12-footer has wooden seats, gunnels, etc., patterned after the original to keep the classic lines. The fiberglass hull offers a virtually maintenance-free boat that can withstand rugged family use; yet the highly finished mahogany work makes this a very distinctive boat. Sails for the 12' are available in gaff or sprit rig.

All of the **WHITEHALLS** are constructed of top quality materials; mahogany seats and gunwales, completely hand laid up fiberglass hull, bronze hardware.

Manufacturer:
B&S Corporation,
Bessey Ridge Rd.,
Albion, ME 04910.
207/437-9245

SPECIFICATIONS:
WHITEHALL
LOA: 12'
Beam: 53"
Weight: 155 lbs.
Sail Area:
  Gaff 78 s.f.
  Sprit 66 s.f.
Approx. Price:
Sail - $2295
Row - $1394

BUTTERFLY

This famous little scow has been in production over 27 years and fleets are located throughout the country. This is the largest scow class in the United States.

The **BUTTERFLY** is a very good choice for the sailor who wants a fast, stable, versatile daysailer the whole family can enjoy.

Because of its scow-type hull, she is a lot more boat than her 12'2" length might indicate. She is agile, and yet can be sailed by two or three. She is the type of boat that can be enjoyed by both the young beginner and the experienced sailor.

Her simple, safe rigging and rugged construction make her an ideal club trainer. Organizations such as camps, Girl and Boy Scouts, and park districts use the **BUTTERFLY** for youth sailing programs.

Manufacturer: Barnett Boat Co., 534 Commercial Avenue, Green Lake, WI 54941. 414/294-6351

SPECIFICATIONS:
BUTTERFLY
LOA: 12'2"
Beam: 54"
Weight: 135 lbs.
Capacity: 600 lbs.
Sail Area: 75 s.f.

Approximate
Price: $1795

BUTTERFLY

ISLANDS 12

The design of the sloop-rigged **ISLANDS 12** is based on traditional lines of a classic sailboat, which has been proven over the years to be superb for all around sailing in light airs or heavy weather. Its high freeboard and the molded-in-place foam for level flotation provide

complete safety. It is also equipped with a fiberglass centerboard, rather than the daggerboard usually found on boats of this size, thus improved handling and safety.

ISLANDS 12

Dry storage space is available in the large compartment under the forward deck.

She is constructed of hand laid up fiberglass bonded together with foam filled compartments for positive flotation. The kick-up rudder blade of 3/16" anodized aluminum is mounted between marine plywood cheeks, fitted with s.s. hardware and a hardwood tiller. Spars are of anodized aluminum, and stays and accessories are stainless.

Fine workmanship, beautiful design and durable construction are all qualities of ISLANDS 12. Gunwale is "U" shaped channel of extra sturdy construction and will resist damage from bumping docksides. The cockpit is deep and roomy, so the boat can be sailed with four adults. Her centerboard trunk is compact. The board with moderate draft provides ample lateral plane.

Her sail plan is simple and easy. It is properly proportioned for good windward ability, as well as running and reaching. Sails are of quality DuPont Dacron, available in multicolor or white.

Rowing stations can be provided so that she can be rowed. This includes a stowable seat, easily installed over the centerboard trunk and spanning the space between the built-in seats. If desired, an outboard motor can be mounted on the transom without a bracket.

Manufacturer: Sumner Boat Company, Inc., 334 S. Bayview Avenue, Amityville, NY 11701. 516/264-1830

SPECIFICATIONS: ISLANDS 12'
LOA: 12'2", Beam: 4'11", Draft: board up 6", board down 2'6", Depth amidship: 20.75", Weight: 250 lbs., Max. H.P.: 5, Capacity: 677 lbs. (5 persons), Total Weight Capacity: 712 lbs., Sail Area: Jib 27 s.f., Main 58 s.f.

Approximate Price: Sailing model: $1995.

TINY CAT

TINY CAT is a plywood version of the original **Beetle Cat.** Designed by Philip Bolger and offered by Harold H. "Dynamite" Payson, the **TINY CAT** uses "tack and tape" construction. This reduces cost and allows for home construction by the amateur builder.

You can purchase this nimble and sea-kindly cat boat ready to sail or order plans for $35.00 from Harold and build it yourself for under $1000 (including sail). Harold also has available many other fine designs and offers a catalogue of study plans for only $3.00.

Manufacturer: Harold H. Payson, Pleasant Beach Road, So. Thomaston, ME 04858. 207/594-7587

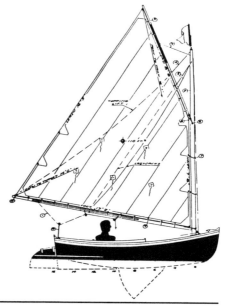

SPECIFICATIONS:
TINY CAT
LOA: 12'3"
Beam: 6'
Draft: 2'9"
Weight: 250 lbs.
Sail Area: 110 s.f.

Approximate
Price: $3200.

Almighty God, we would let no day pass without prayer. Help us to so temper our lives that we will not be tempestuous; to be so big that we will not be thrown from our course by little matters. Thou art the pilot of our lives and with our trust in Thee we are ever ready for what the day may bring forth. Amen.

TINY CAT

BARNSTABLE CAT BOAT

John Howard has been building boats in Barnstable, Massachusetts for 49 years. He specializes in smaller hulls and has been providing the **BARNSTABLE CAT BOAT** since 1983.

This cat boat is a fiberglass version of the old original **Beetle Cat** that has been so famous in the Massachusetts area.

With her oak and cedar trim, fir spars, and bronze hardware, she is a classic looking daysailer.

Manufacturer: John G. Howard, Jr. Boats, Barnstable, Massachusetts 02630. 617/362-6859

SPECIFICATIONS: BARNSTABLE CAT BOAT
LOA: 12'4", LWL: 11'8", Beam: 6', Weight: 420 lbs., Draft: board up 6", board down 2', Sail Area: 100 s.f.

Approximate Price: $5275.

BEETLE CAT

First designed and built in 1921 by the Beetle family in New Bedford, Massachusetts, over 2000 of these great boats have been produced since.

This is the **"ORIGINAL BEETLE CAT BOAT"**, an ideal boat for learning to sail or for anyone looking for a roomy, small daysailer that will give many years of safe and comfortable sailing. If you're in New England, there are regattas sponsored by the class association.

This classic is still manufactured the original way, and the Concordia Co. urges customers and friends to visit the old boat shop to see these beautiful dinghies being formed.

Class Association: New England Beetle Cat Boat Association, 40 Juniper Road, Holbrook, MA 02343.

Manufacturer: Concordia Company, Inc., South Wharf, P.O. Box P203, South Dartmouth, Massachusetts, 02748. 617/996-9971

SPECIFICATIONS:
ORIGINAL
BEETLE CAT
BOAT
LOA: 12'4"
LWL: 11'8"
Beam: 6'
Draft:
  board down 2'
Weight: 450 lbs.
Sail Area: 100 s.f.

**Approximate
Price:** $5335

BEETLE CAT
Photo by: Norman Fortier

PUFFER

If you're looking for a basic sailboat that can bring the fun of sailing to the whole family, take a good look at **PUFFER**. She's a beautifully designed sloop that proves that a safe, reliable boat can deliver a lot of sailing satisfaction. **PUFFER** gives you the stability of a strong, wide hull, daysailing comfort for three adults, and the built-in safety of full foam flotation.

PUFFER also offers the promise of years of versatile boating for the whole family. **PUFFER** can be sailed, rowed or powered with a small outboard. She comes fully equipped with mainsail and jib, anodized aluminum mast and boom, and oar locks. **PUFFER** has brightly varnished mahogany board and rudder, stainless steel rigging and gleaming smooth fiberglass hull with accent stripe.

Manufacturer: Alcort Sailboats, Inc., South Leonard St., Waterbury, CT 06708. 203/756-7091

SPECIFICATIONS:
PUFFER
LOA: 12'6:
Beam: 4'10"
Weight: 160 lbs.
Capacity: 450 lbs.
Sail Area:
 Main 55 s.f.
 Jib 35 s.f.

Approximate
Price: $2200.

We thank Thee, our heavenly Father, for health which enables us to do our daily duties. Grant us strength to stand for right and faith to see the battle through. Amen.

PUFFER

MISTRAL 12

Ideal family sailing! The **MISTRAL 12** can accommodate up to five persons in a spacious cockpit area. Conceived as a multi-purpose sailboat, it can be sailed, rowed or powered by a small outboard motor.

Two large storage compartments, with locking clasps, provide ample space for sails and oars.

The **MISTRAL 12** can safely and easily be sailed by the most inexperienced sailor as length, beam, depth and displacement enhances stability.

Although designed for family sailing, **MISTRAL 12** also offers unequaled sailing performance as the novice gains experience.

The **MISTRAL 12**, synonymous with family boating, is a multi-purpose craft which can be enjoyed by all.

Manufacturer: Canadian Yacht Builders, P.O. Box 67, Dorion, Quebec, Canada J7V 5V8. 514/455-6183

SPECIFICATIONS: MISTRAL 12
LOA: 12'6", LWL: 11'8", Beam: 4'10", Draft: Centerboard up 6", Centerboard down 3'4", Weight: 200 lbs., Sail Area: Main 70 s.f., Jib 25 s.f.

Approximate Price: $2777

DYER DHOW

Beauty and strength are two of the qualities synonymous with the 12 1/2' **DYER DHOW**. This is the largest
in the line of **Dyer** dinghies. She is hand-built, which
has produced a dinghy that is light but unusually strong

and durable. This beautiful dinghy stands up under
heavy use, and she performs uniquely whether you sail it,
row it, tow it or power it with a small outboard.

DYER DHOW

Dyer dinghies were first built over a half century ago, using wood for construction. Now they are being constructed of fiberglass, but also have quality materials like oak, mahogany and teak. Only the very best rigging and hardware are used on the **DYER DHOW**, producing a dinghy a somewhat more expensive than the average, but with far greater durability than the average.

The **DYER DHOW** is a smart investment, if you want a dinghy with true quality, true craftsmanship and durability.

Manufacturer: The Anchorage, Inc., 57 Miller Street, Warren, Rhode Island 02885-0403. 401/245-3300

SPECIFICATIONS:
DYER DHOW
LOA: 151 1/2"
Beam: 62 3/8"
Depth: 25 5/8"
Draft:
 board up 7.75"
 down 47.25"
Hull Wt.: 220 lbs.
Capacity: 1025 lbs

Approximate
Price: $3950

As we retire to our beds for rest unto our bodies, we turn to Thee for rest unto our souls, O Lord. We are not tired by labor but restless with anxiety and uncertainty. May the calm of Thy spirit smooth the rough seas of our lives and give us refuge from all the cross currents and winds. We are thine, O God, and we shall trust in Thee. Amen.

PEAPOD

The **PEAPOD** design is over 200 years old. The mold for this one came from a restored antique hull in Maine. HiLiner has been building these for over 10 years. She can be sailed with the oars stowed under the seats or rowed with her mast under the seats.

She is an excellent sailer, very stiff for a small boat. This is attributed to her loose footed 3/4 fractional rig having a low center of effort. Board down, she only draws 24" draft and centerboard and rudder are kick-up beaching.

The double-ended hull creates less drag and makes her one of the finest rowing boats available. This hull also makes her a great tender that is not effected by following seas. She will carry a large load and stability increases as weight is added. She can handle a 2 H.P. engine on the side rail. The **PEAPOD** is a beautiful dinghy with all mahogany trim and, at only 120 lbs., is easily transported and launched.

Manufacturer:
HiLiner Marine,
P.O. Box P-73,
South Dartmouth,
MA 02748.
617/992-1807

SPECIFICATIONS:
PEAPOD
LOA: 12'10"
Beam: 4'1"
Draft:
  board up 4"
  board down 24"
Weight: 120 lbs.
Sail Area: 82 s.f.

Approx. Price:
Row - $950
Sail - $1695

STARWING

There are other dinghies that offer sailing/rowing conversions. But, the **STARWING** is different. One realizes it is unique at first sight. Its extended side deck "wings" make the boat roomy, as well as add performance and stability for sailing.

For rowing, the wings are the support for the optional rowing rig. And "rowing", doesn't mean a couple of oars and oarlocks. It means an Olympic-regulation sliding seat and rowing equipment, designed by an Olympic rower.

STARWING was designed by master designer Jim Kyle and his design partner, Lisa Hicks. It is built to strict specifications out of hand-laid fiberglass. All wood is mahogany, and all hardware is Harken and Dwyer.

The wing-flared topsides keep the boat on its feet in heavy winds and provide an added safety margin by resisting capsizing and let you re-right the boat quickly. The **STARWING** sails well as a cat rig or under main and jib. There is a lot built into this 13-footer.

Manufacturer: Starwing, Inc., P.O. Box 137, Bristol, RI 02809. 401/254-0670

SPECIFICATIONS:
STARWING
LOA: 12'11"
Beam: 63"
Draft:
 board up 34"
 board down 3'
Hull Wt.: 160 lbs.
Sail Area:
 Main: 70 s.f.
 Jib: (optional) 35 s.f.
Capacity: 3 adults

Approximate
Price: $2400.

STARWING

ZUMA

The **ZUMA** is a sporty looking, inexpensive and easy to sail dinghy. This is a very good first boat for both adult and youth sailor. The sleeved mainsail keeps the rigging very simple, but the addition of a halyard allows for rapid lowering of the sail. This is a definite safety advantage over sleeved designs that do not contain this feature.

The **ZUMA's** five foot beam and hard chine provide good stability. With Alcort quality and all low maintenance materials, this boat should provide the beginning sailor with a lot of hassle-free, fun sailing.

Class Association: Zuma Class Association, Alcort Sailboats, Inc., P.O. Box 1345, Waterbury, CT 06725.

Manufacturer: Alcort Sailboats, Inc., P.O. Box 1345, Waterbury, CT 06725. 203/756-7091

SPECIFICATIONS:
ZUMA
LOA: 12'11"
LWL: 12'5"
Draft:
 board up 4"
 board down 26"
Beam: 5'
Mast height above
 water: 18'
Sail area: 65 s.f.
Luff length: 14'6"
Cockpit length:
 4'9"
Hull weight: 127
 lbs.
Capacity: 500 lbs.

**Approximate
Price:** $1295.

ZUMA

BAY SAILER

Classic Marine has introduced their new 13' **BAY SAILER**. Built in the traditional lapstrake style of their sailing dinghies, she features the beautiful woodwork finishing that has become the Classic Marine trademark.

She will sail four in comfort and comes with all the features of the **Classic 8' and 10'**. La Playa styling, including solid teak trim and recessed rope gunnel guard, customize the **BAY SAILER**.

BAY SAILER

Manufacturer: Classic Marine, 2244 Main St., Ste. 3, Chula Vista, California 92011. 619/423-0206

SPECIFICATIONS:
BAY SAILER
LOA: 13'
Beam: 5'6"
Mast: 19'
Sail Area: 91 s.f.
Weight: 150 lbs.

Approximate
Price:
Classic - $1895.
La Playa - $2295.

CYCLONE 13

For one of the best in high performance one design single-handed racing or lively daysailing for two, try the **CYCLONE 13**.

Successfully combining the best features in its class with high quality construction and hardware make the **CYCLONE 13** the outstanding choice in her class.

The hull and deck are sturdy, hand laminated fiberglass that is easy to maintain and light enough to car top. She has a unique mast with forestay and halyard that allows the sail to be lowered without unrigging, a kick-up rudder and daggerboard that make beaching easy.

The **CYCLONE 13** features molded in waterline stripes, teak trim and very complete standard equipment, making the **CYCLONE** a quality leader.

Class Association: Cyclone National Association, c/o The Boat Works, 28710 Canwood Street, #107, Agoura Hills, CA 91367. 818/991-0540

Manufacturer: Capri Sailboats, 21200 Victory Boulevard, Woodland Hills, CA 91367. 818/884-7700

SPECIFICATIONS: CYCLONE 13
LOA: 13', Beam: 4'11", Weight: 148 lbs., Sail Area: 74 s.f.

Approximate Price: $1695

For Our Mailmen

Dear Lord, we ask Thy blessing upon our shipmates who work in the Ship's Post Office. We are grateful for their untiring and selfless endeavors in securing and distributing the mail. We also ask that Thou would be especially near to any of our shipmates who may have received bad news from home. O God, watch over us this day. Amen.

CYCLONE 13

CODE 40

The **CODE 40**, born of the latest refinements in sailing technology, was created by Andre Cornu -- with all the professional perfectionism for which he is renowned.

Because of the sophistication of its superstructure and its remarkable lightness, the **CODE 40** will surprise even the expert sailor with its fleetness and sensitive handling. It will plane beautifully in moderate wind condition and, not only is the **CODE 40** designed for competition, it also excels as a safe, comfortable pleasure craft. Its hull is rimmed with seats which are airtight, unsinkable flotation chambers as well. The **CODE 40** is crafted in Canada to meet your needs at a very reasonable cost.

Manufacturer: C&L Boatworks, 884 Dillingham Rd., Pickering, Ontario, Canada L1W 1Z6. 416/839-7991

SPECIFICATIONS: CODE 40
LOA: 13.1', Beam: 5.1', Max. Wt.: 187 lbs., Draft: board down - 3.3', Sail Area: 108 s.f., Mast Ht. on Deck: 18.9'.

Approximate Price: $3140 (Canadian Currency).

CODE 40

PRECISION 13

Aggressive, spirited performance is not a characteristic that one would normally associate with an economical purchase price. That, however, is exactly what the **PRECISION 13** was designed to deliver.

She combines a simple unstayed cat rig with a sleek modern hull shape. It is a simple fun boat whose light weight makes it easy to get on plane and yet stable and forgiving for the beginner. Don't let her good manners fool you, however. With an experienced skipper at the helm, she can perform with the best of them and give you the maximum amount of enjoyment for your dollar.

The **PRECISION 13** can be car-topped or trailered to your favorite spot and can be easily carried by two people. She comes standard with top notch hardware and running gear. If you're looking for a small, fast, fun boat, check out this Steven Seaton design.

Manufacturer: Precision Boat Works, 8517 Bradenton Road, Sarasota, FL 34243. 813/758-5611

SPECIFICATIONS:
PRECISION 13
LOA: 13'2"
Beam: 4'8"
Draft:
  board up 4"
  board down 2'8"
Sail Area: 85 s.f.
Weight: 140 lbs.

Approximate
Price: $1500.

PRECISION 13

INTERNATIONAL FJ

Formerly called the **Flying Junior**, this represents one of the best small sailboats on the market. The **INTERNATIONAL FJ** has many features not offered in most dinghies her size, and at an affordable price.

The **FJ** gives it all to you from the beginning to the end. You can sail under main and jib to start, and move right up to the spinnaker when you are ready. With the **FJ**, you won't get bored soon after you learn to sail. The spinnaker makes down-wind work fun and adds to the excitement for the crew.

The class association is long established and well organized. Your **FJ** will never be out of date, and you will be able to enjoy the competition of class racing across the country.

Sharp looking, fast and easy to manage on the water or on a trailer -- the **FJ** is a great little boat!

Class Association: International FJ Class Association, Steve Klotz, National President, 3379 Brittan Avenue, No. 10, San Carlos, CA 94070.

Manufacturer: Diversified Composites, 208 Prospect Northeast, Blairstown, Iowa 52209. 319/454-6264

Manufacturer: H & H Sailcraft, Rt. 1, Box 6, New Paris, Ohio 45347. 513/437-7261

SPECIFICATIONS:
INTERNATIONAL FJ
LOA: 13'3"
Beam: 5'3"
Hull Wt.: 165 lbs.
Sail Area:
  Main 64 s.f.
  Jib 36 s.f.
  Spinnaker 80 s.f.

Approximate Price: $3200.

INTERNATIONAL FJ

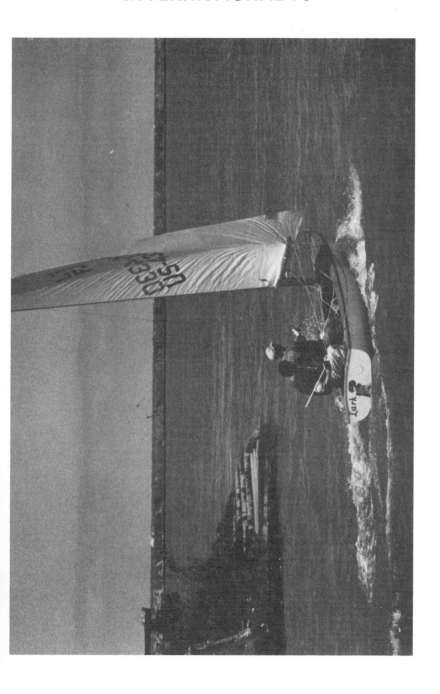

MISTRAL 4.04

The **MISTRAL 4.04** has it all. She makes learning to sail easy, provides great enjoyment for pleasure sailing, and is very suited to competition racing. Sturdiness, durability and easy maintenance are integral features of the **4.04**.

It can be said that the **MISTRAL 4.04** has contributed generously to the sport of sailing in terms of initiating newcomers as well as helping many to sharpen their sailing skill, escalating the popularity of the sport, as well as to improve upon technical aspects.

Manufactured for over ten years, the **MISTRAL 4.04** has become the choice of a majority of schools, associations, resort areas and leisure sailing enthusiasts.

Manufacturer: Canadian Yacht Builders, P.O. Box 67, Dorion, Quebec, Canada J7V, 5V8. 514/455-6183

SPECIFICATIONS: MISTRAL 4.04
LOA: 13'3", LWL: 12', Beam: 4'9", Draft: Centerboard up 6", Centerboard down 3'6", Sail Area: Main 75 s.f., Jib 25 s.f., Spinnaker 155 s.f., Weight: 175 lbs.

Approximate Price: $2779.

SPINDRIFT

SPINDRIFT sailing is exciting and exhilarating. Swift and light as the spray off the waves, she's designed to plane easily, yet with her hard chine hull she's stable. And, with her unsinkable design, she's equally as safe in the hands of the enthusiastic novice as she is with the experienced racing helmsman.

The **SPINDRIFT** comes complete with mainsail (with reef points), jib, mast, boom and all stainless steel rigging, centerboard and kick-up rudder -- there's even a built-in insulated cooler.

SPINDRIFT has been the choice of almost a thousand sailors throughout North America.

Manufacturer: Vandestadt & McGruer Ltd., Yacht Designers & Builders, P.O. Box 7, Owen Sound, Ontario Canada N4K 5P1. 519/376-8548

SPECIFICATIONS:
SPINDRIFT
LOA: 13'4"
Beam: 5'2"
Draft:
  board up 4"
  board down 3'
Weight: 205 lbs.
Sail Area: 100 s.f.

Approximate
Price: $2295

Touch our lips, O God, and sweeten our speech that we may not profane any compartment on this ship nor make unclean any fellowship. Make us know that we shall give account of every idle word spoken. Enable us to be a credit and not a debit in the ledger of our ship's log. Amen.

BLUE JAY

The **BLUE JAY** was designed by Sparkman & Stevens in 1946 as a Jr. **Lightning**, with her primary purpose as a junior training boat. She is a very good trainer and daysailer, because she carries main, jib and spinnaker.

While her rig is short, she is lively and fast and ghosts along easily in light air. Her cockpit is roomy and her beam and shallow "V" bottom provide amazing stiffness. The **BLUE JAY** is well balanced, responsive and easily trailered and rigged. She is a fine all-around racer or daysailer.

She offers a well organized class with over 6500 boats and approximately 150 fleets in North America. The class boasts the **BLUE JAY** to be the *"biggest little One Design sloop of her size afloat today"*. Check it out, they may be right.

Class Association: Blue Jay Class Association, Box 651, Mantoloking, New Jersey 08738.

Manufacturer: Saybrook Yacht Yard, Old Lyme, CT 06731. 203/434-7025

SPECIFICATIONS:
BLUE JAY
LOA: 13'6"
Beam: 5'2"
Draft:
  board up 6"
  board down 3'8"
Weight (rigged):
  275 lbs.
Sail Area:
  main 90 s.f.
  jib 28 s.f.

Approximate
Price: $4200.

BLUE JAY

Photo by: Mitch Carucci

JEZEBELE

The **JEZEBELE** is the daysailer for young and old alike. Her hard chine makes her an excellent trainer. No fancy hardware or complicated rigging. Simple to rig and simple to sail. Her roomy cockpit provides comfort for four. Her extra depth keeps children dry and safe. Flotation filled compartments make her unsinkable. She carries anodized spars, Dacron sails and mahogany rudder, tiller and centerboard.

Every Ensign Dinghy is built to the high quality standards of Mike Dapice, founder of Ensign Dinghies and Marine. Coremat construction assures strength as well as a lightweight hull. All hull fittings are backed by hardwood plates. Seats are molded in or solid mahogany. Interior and exterior is gelcoated for beauty as well as easy cleanup.

Manufacturer: Ensign Dinghies & Marine, Michael Dapice Enterprises, Inc., P.O. Box 547, Rye, NY 10580. 914/967-1656

SPECIFICATIONS:
JEZEBELE
LOA: 13'6"
Beam: 5'4"
Depth: 20"
Sail Area: 90 s.f.
Weight: 165 lbs.
Capacity: 600 lbs.
Max. H.P.: 9.6

Approximate Price: $2000

CAPRI 13

The **CAPRI 13** is simple for a beginner or junior sailor to rig and handle, yet sophisticated enough to satisfy experienced small boat sailors.

With input from great sailors around the world, the **CAPRI 13** was designed with a comfortable deck design, sleek styling and a controllable high performance rig. She planes quickly and delivers great upwind performance. The beam and firm bilges offer stability on and off the wind. First class hardware and rigging add up to lasting quality for the **CAPRI 13**.

Class Association: Capri 13 Class Association, P.O. Box 989, Woodland Hills, CA 91367.

Manufacturer: Capri Sailboats, 21200 Victory Blvd., Woodland Hills, CA 91367. 818/884-7700

SPECIFICATIONS: CAPRI 13
LOA: 13'8", Beam: 4'8", Weight: 128 lbs., Sail Area: 72 s.f.
Approximate Price: $1500

HOLDER 14 MKII

This is a great family daysailer. The **HOLDER 14 MKII** is one of the roomiest and most comfortable daysailers available in this size range. There is plenty of room for the cooler, picnic and family.

She looks good and is responsive, yet she is very sturdy and stable. My family and I have spent many enjoyable days in this fine, easy to sail pleasure from **Hobie Cat**. We have owned many daysailers, but this is one of our favorites.

HOLDER 14 MKII, designed by Ron Holder, will give you years of fun and maintain her value when you want to change to another class or move up to a bigger boat.

Class Association: Holder 14 Class Association, P.O. Box 1008, Oceanside, CA 92054.

Manufacturer: Hobie Cat, P.O. Box 1008, Oceanside, CA 92054. 619/758-9100

SPECIFICATIONS:
HOLDER 14 MKII
LOA: 13'8"
LWL: 12'6"
Beam: 6'2"
Weight: 265 lbs.
Sail Area:
  Main 75 s.f.
  Jib 35 s.f.
Draft:
  board up 6"
  board down 3'10"

Approximate
Price: $2490.

HOLDER 14 MKII

AQUA FINN

Designed for the inexperienced sailor or the novice seeking sailing performance and simplicity, the **AQUA FINN** is ideal for training or rental.

AQUA FINN, now in production for eight years, is a direct competitor of the **Sunfish** and offers many great features. She has features not available in other competitive sport daysailers of this size and price range. The cockpit is large enough to accommodate two adults with a built-in hiking strap and includes a DePersia cockpit bailer. The hulls include positive foam flotation for safety.

Manufacturer: American Sail, Inc., 7350 Pepperdam Avenue, Pepperdam Industrial Park, Charleston, South Carolina 29418. 803/552-8548

SPECIFICATIONS:
AQUA FINN
LOA: 13'9"
Beam: 4'2"
Draft:
 board up 4"
 board down 34"
Hull Weight:
 125 lbs.
Sail Area: 75 s.f.
Crew Capacity:
 500 lbs.

**Approximate
Price:** $1245.

Spare us from the realization that we have wasted the hours of this day. There is so much need for faith, love and friendship. Forgive any idle word which may have caused hurt to a shipmate. As we close our eyes in sleep, we breathe a prayer for our loved ones. Amen.

AQUA FINN

INTERNATIONAL 420

This fine racing one-design is one of the most popular in the world. Over 40,000 have been produced and over 35,000 are racing today.

Designed in France by Christian Maury, in the late 50's, the **420** gained popularity quickly around the world. It is one of the very best choices for the sailor just getting into racing or anyone looking for something between a slow daysailing dinghy and the very difficult to sail Olympic racer. The **420** is an outstanding racer for the young or lighter crew. The **420** can even be raced/sailed single-handed and easily self-rescued.

The class has an impressive racing record which includes two World Championships, the Women's World

INTERNATIONAL 420

Championship and a complete sweep of U.S. and North American Championships.

The **420** Class Association is strong and well-organized. It offers many regattas, a good newsletter and worldwide sailing possibilities.

This is the type of dinghy you can push to the limit, hanging out on a trapeze with spinnaker flying, or take out for a lazy day sail.

Class Association: US 420 Class Association, Ron Breault, President, 162 Four Mile River Rd., Old Lyme, Connecticut 06371.
Manufacturer: Vanguard Racing Sailboats, 79 Joyce Street, Warren, Rhode Island 02885. 401/245-8608

SPECIFICATIONS: 420
LOA: 13'9", LWL: 13'2", Beam: 5'5", Draft: board up 6", board down 3'2", Sail Area: 110 s.f., Spinnaker: 95 s.f., Hull Weight: 176 lbs.   **Approximate Price: $5350**

PRECISION 14

For exceptional responsiveness and shear exhilaration, a small, lightweight sailboat is truly hard to beat. The **PRECISION 14** was designed by Steve Seaton to offer you all of that and more.

She is an excellent first choice for the novice sailor. The basics become easy to understand because the boat tells you instantly when it needs attention. Her ample beam gives her the stability to make her a forgiving partner while you gain experience. If you really want her to go, however, hold on! The **PRECISION 14** offers high spirited sailing performance whether you're headed across the pond or around the race course. It is because of this versatility that fleets of **PRECISION 14**'s are growing rapidly around the country. Like her sisters, you won't find any skimping on quality here. Harken blocks, Samson Braid, Dwyer Spars, Elvstrom designed bailers and more are the equipment you find on winners.

She comes standard with high kick-up rudder and a large storage locker forward as well as the very best hardware and running gear.

Manufacturer: Precision Boat works, 8517 Bradenton Road, Sarasota, FL 34243. 813/758-5611

SPECIFICATIONS:
PRECISION 14
LOA: 13'10"
Beam: 6'1"
Draft:
 board up 5"
 board down 2'9"
Sail Area: 129 s.f.
Weight: 250 lbs.

Approximate
Price: $2100.

PRECISION 14

SUNFISH

More people have sailed on it, learned on it, raced on it and spent a relaxed sunny afternoon on it than any other fiberglass sailboat ever built.

There's never been a better beginner's boat; forgiving to the novice with plenty of challenge in store as your skills develop. In less than a week, you'll be a SUNFISH sailor, turning ordinary weekends into adventures.

Over 230,000 SUNFISH have been sold since the first one was launched over a quarter of a century ago. Thousands of organized SUNFISH regattas are held every year -- from fun-filled river races to the annual World Championship. SUNFISH sailors enjoy a whole world of sailing and social activities, as SUNFISH is the largest one-design racing class in the world, and growing daily.

FORTUNE magazine called the SUNFISH "one of the 25 best-designed products in America." And, in a poll of nearly half a million readers of SAIL, it was called "the breakthrough board boat."

Weekdays, weekends -- anytime and anyplace is the perfect time for SUNFISH sailing. You can cartop it anywhere, even on a sub-compact. And it stores as easily as it transports.

SUNFISH, it's got enough spirit to challenge the sailor in you for many years.

Class Association: International Sunfish Class Association, 1413 Capella S., Newport, RI 02840.

Manufacturer: Alcort Sailboats, Inc., P.O. Box 1345, South Leonard St., Waterbury, Connecticut 06725. 203/756-7091

SPECIFICATIONS: SUNFISH
Length: 13'10", Beam: 4'1", Sail Area: 75 s.f., Hull Weight: 129 lbs., Capacity: 500 lbs. (1-4) **Approximate Price:** $1395.

SUNFISH

FORCE 5

What is a **FORCE 5**? A powerful single-handed *racing machine* with a cockpit big enough for two. Fourteen feet of *sailing machine* to really challenge your skills.

The deck and hull are made of rigid, light-weight, hand-laid fiberglass. The **FORCE 5** is light-weight, stores easily and car-tops anywhere.

She is an ideal one-design for perfecting your knowledge of sail controls. The **FORCE 5** features quality-made sails, Harken blocks and hexaratchet, 8 part vang, dual outhaul and cunningham, and full-width, mid-cockpit roller bearing traveler -- all standard equipment.

If you're considering a flat-out single hander, be sure to check out **FORCE 5** -- the one that lets you sail up a storm.

Class Association: Force 5 Class Association, Lee Parks, Secretary, 1413 Capella S, Newport, RI 02840.

Manufacturer: Alcort Sailboats, Inc., P.O. Box 1345, South Leonard Street, Waterbury, Connecticut 06725. 203/756-7091

SPECIFICATIONS:
FORCE 5
LOA: 13'10.5"
Beam: 4'10"
Draft:
 board up 5.5"
 board down 2'10"
Hull Weight: 145 lbs.
 fully rigged 160 lbs.
Sail Area: 91 s.f.
Crew Capacity:
 500 lbs.
 1-3 people

Approximate Price: $2095

FORCE 5

LASER

The famous **LASER** made its debut over 15 years ago. Over 130,000 have been produced since then. This hot little design by Bruce Kirby is one of the best.

The sales literature claims "You'll never forget your first **LASER**." I must agree. I was first introduced to this sporty dinghy while sailing my home-made catamaran at a beautiful little beach on the West coast of Japan. It was very light air that day, and I was lying on the tramp, using a life jacket for a pillow when this small orange dinghy went past me. At first, I attributed this to my not minding my trim, so I sat up, sheeted in, and

attempted to catch him. After a few minutes, he jibed and came back and pulled alongside. I admired his boat, so he offered to trade, as he would also like to try my cat. I was amazed at the responsiveness and handling ease. Even a hint of a puff seemed to send it scooting. I will always remember that day. I purchased my own some years later in the States.

LASER

LASERS can be purchased in a Radial model or can be simply converted by purchasing a smaller, specially cut sail and lower mast sections. The **LASER RADIAL** allows the lightweight sailor to compete on equal terms with heavier sailors. The conversion is great when adults and youngsters might use the same boat. The Radial rig can also be raised/lowered with a halyard, for greater safety.

When you buy a **LASER**, you will automatically become a member of the International Laser Class Association. The ILCA is a worldwide community of **LASER** owners who sail in regattas from local races all the way up to World Class competition. A strong organization of volunteers organize owners into regions. Districts and Fleets provide competitions for all levels of sailors from Grand Masters (age 55 and over) to Youths, Women's and Light Weight divisions.

Class Association: International Laser Class Association, Fiona Kidd, P.O. Box 569, Hawkesbury, Ontario, Canada K6A 3C8. 613/632-4415

Manufacturer: Laser International, 1250 Tessier St., Hawkesbury, Ontario, Canada K6A 3C8. 613/632-1181

SPECIFICATIONS:
LASER
LOA: 13'10.5"
LWL: 12'6"
Beam: 4'6"
Hull Weight:
  130 lbs.
Sail Area:
  130 s.f.
Sail Area (**Radial**):
  62 s.f.

Approximate
Price: $2150

DINGHIES AND DAYSAILERS /
14' To 15.99'

CAPRI 14

The **CAPRI 14** is a terrific family daysailer, and just as lively and fun to sail as her famous cousin, the **Lido 14**. Beautiful, but rugged and durable, the hull and deck are one piece, hand laid up fiberglass and built to yield strength and rigidity.

A 250 lb. fiberglass encased, cast lead keel gives great stability. The shallow draft makes it very easy to beach the boat and sail in very shallow water.

Hardware for the **CAPRI** includes gold anodized aluminum bow fitting to hold the jib stay turnbuckle and jib tack shackle. The gold anodized mast hinge makes raising and lower the mast very easy.

The boom vang comes equipped with roller bearing block and a two-part outhaul. There is also an optional whisker pole available.

Manufacturer: W.D. Schock Corp., 3502 South Greenville Street, Santa Ana, CA 92704-7095. 714/549-2277

SPECIFICATIONS:
CAPRI 14
LOA: 14'
Beam: 6'
Draft: 2'2"
Sail Area: 110 s.f.
Weight: 400 lbs.

Approximate
Price: $2775.

CAPRI 14

HANDY CAT 14

The **HANDY CAT 14** is a dry, safe, comfortable daysailer with traditional cat boat lines and proportions which will appeal to lovers of little yachts with character. For comfortable big cockpit day sailing, it's hard to beat a classic cat.

She is easily trailerable, and her shoal draft and inherent stability make her an excellent boat for family fun. The **HANDY CAT** is constructed of fine materials such as burnished bronze hardware and blocks, Sitka spruce spars, teak trim, etc.

The **HANDY CAT** boasts more cockpit space than a thirty-footer, and has one of the easiest and most practical rigs for a boat this size. Her simple rigging includes just a headstay for standing rig and peak and throat halyards, as well as a main sheet for running rigging. There are no jib sheet winches to tend, no expensive gear to add to maker her go. Just lower the board, peak up the main and cast off.

HANDY CAT's classic proportions are evident, even as she rests at the mooring...from her plumb stern along her beautiful sheer to a transom which brings to mind fine old sailing yachts.

Manufacturer: Nauset Marine Sailboats, Route 6A, Orleans, MA 02653. 617/255-0777

SPECIFICATIONS: HANDY CAT 14
LOA: 14', Beam: 6'8", Draft: board up - 12", board down - 54", Sail Area: 141 s.f., Displacement: 750 lbs.

Approximate Price: $7000.

HANDY CAT 14

INTERNATIONAL 14

This is the original International Yacht Racing Union dinghy. The **INTERNATIONAL 14** was the first true planing class. The class began in the early 1920's and gained International status in 1928.

Pinnacle Design's International 14

This class is responsible for many, if not most, of the development of dinghy design to date. Unlike a one-design class, this class not only allows improvements, it encourages them. This has produced a state-of-the-art 14 foot planing dinghy.

One of the most recent developments in the class has led to an asymmetric mast head spinnaker and retractable 9-foot spinnaker pole. The Canadian fleet is currently allowing in developing these trends.

You can build or purchase the boat in any material you like. Most are cold moulded wood or fiberglass. Boats are being vacuum bagged using PVC foam for core. Current trends have also led to double trapezes. The rules for the class are simple and clear. The basic specification limitations are length, beam, hull weight and crew size. There are many more subtle rules, but there is room for the owner to experiment almost everywhere.

INTERNATIONAL 14

Ontario Yachts is now offering a tamer version of the **14** called the **B-14**. This development is an inter-collegiate class, and differs from the **14** in rig size. It sports a fraction rig asymmetric spinnaker, a shorter retractable pole and a single trap. ($6700 FOB warehouse)

All **INTERNATIONAL 14**'s are thoroughbreds. If you are looking for a nice easy to sail daysailer, look around. If you want to race, want equipment and want to go fast, check this one out.

Ontario Yachts' Asymmetrical Mast Head International 14

Class Association: U.S. International 14 Association, Rod Mincher, 7 Edelmar Drive, Annapolis, MD 21403.

Manufacturer: Pinnacle Design Group, 550 Maple Avenue, Carpinteria, CA 93013. 805/684-6680

Manufacturer: Ontario Yachts, 243 Speers Road, Oakville, Ontario, Canada L6K 2E8. 416/845-1153

SPECIFICATIONS: INTERNATIONAL 14
LOA: 14' (max.), Beam: 5.5' (max.), Hull: 200 lbs. (min.), Crew: Two   **Approx. Price: $9700**

LIDO 14

This beautiful 14-foot sloop began as the cat-rigged **Lehman 14**, a relatively uncomfortable daggerboard boat, designed by **Star** sailor Barney Lehman. After purchasing Lehman's boat building concern, W.D. "Bill" Schock used this 14-foot design as the starting point of what would become a smart looking centerboard sloop with excellent racing capabilities and all the comforts needed for family sailing. He modified the hull design, added contoured bench seats and a large deck with a molded splash rail, and finished it to "yacht" standards not yet seen in small sailboats.

This unique design hit the marketplace in 1958 when the only small one-design sailboats available were hot racing boats like the **Star, Thistle** and **International 14**. These boats required considerable skill and lots of athletic ability. Bill Schock recognized the need for a small sailboat that could be competitively and comfortably

LIDO 14

raced by a husband/wife team. The **LIDO 14** was the perfect answer and met with instant success, seeing the formation of a one-design class association the first year.

One of the most remarkable things about the **LIDO** is that in almost 30 years, only minor modifications have been made in the gear and detailing. The hull, deck, interior and rigging are the same, so many of the first hulls are still out there winning against the new ones.

But, the **LIDO 14** is not used primarily for racing. Most of her owners happily cruise their boats on bays and lakes throughout the U.S. and Mexico. She has been the choice of many college sailing teams and city recreation departments and has also been an extremely popular rental boat.

In 1958, the **LIDO 14** was more innovative than ever imagined. It paved the way for a new era in sailing -- a time when sailing became a family past-time available at affordable prices -- an era to which the **LIDO 14** is still a vital part.

Class Association: Lido 14 Class Association, P.O. Box 1252, Newport Beach, CA 92663.

Manufacturer: W.D. Schock Corp., 3502 South Greenville, Santa Ana, CA 92704. 714/549-2277

SPECIFICATIONS: LIDO 14
LOA: 14'
Beam: 6'
Draft:
  board up 5"
  board down 4'3"
Sail Area: 111 s.f.
Weight: 310 lbs.

Approximate Price: $3000

PINTAIL

The **PINTAIL** is designed to be a versatile racer/daysailer. Many racing classes are built strictly for performance, sacrificing stability and sometimes safety. While the **PINTAIL** is competitive with many classes her size, she also provides a large, dry cockpit for easy family daysailing with safety and stability.

You can race this boat, or just leisurely cruise on the lakes. She can be trailered behind a small car and rigged to sail in just minutes.

PINTAIL is built to last. Marine concepts gives a one year unconditional warranty. All stress points are reinforced, and rigging is high quality. Foam flotation makes her unsinkable. Over 2000 of these fine boats have been produced.

Manufacturer: Marine Concepts, 159 Oakwood Street East, Tarpon Springs, FL 34689. 813/937-0166

SPECIFICATIONS:
PINTAIL
LOA: 14'
Beam: 6'
Draft:
 board up 6"
 board down 3'9"
Sail Area: main
 & jib 135 s.f.
Mast Height: (keel
 to masthead) 23'
Weight: (fully
 rigged) 400 lbs.

Approximate
Price: $2600

PINTAIL

CAPRI 14.2

An excellent choice for those looking for a good family daysailer, and active one-design racing for the young an old alike, this is the **CAPRI 14.2**.

She is very stable, simply rigged and has one of the most comfortable cockpits of any dinghy in this size range. We have been known to nap on the comfortable seats during light winds.

The **CAPRI 14.2** is ideal for today's lifestyle. She is very quick and easy to rig and trailers behind a small car. She's good looking and very easy to maintain. The retracting centerboard and kick-up rudder are great for beaching. There's plenty of room for the cooler and all the paraphernalia for a picnic.

I have always felt the **CAPRI 14.2** was a very good starter boat because of her handling characteristics. Her wide beam gives good stability, and her softer chine allows the new sailor to experience keeling without the abrupt change in heeling attitude felt with harder chines.

Class Association: Capri 14.2 National Association P.O. Box 3161, Westlake Village, CA 91359.

Manufacturer: Capri Sailboats, 21200 Victory Blvd., Woodland Hills, CA 91367. 818/884-7700

SPECIFICATIONS:
CAPRI 14.2
LOA: 14'2"
Beam: 6'2"
Sail Area: 114 s.f.
Draft:
 board up 4"
 board down 3'6"
Weight: 340 lbs.

Approximate
Price: $2300

CAPRI 14.2

CL 14

Some of the outstanding characteristics of the **CL 14** are her double-chine hull, deep open cockpit and unsinkable hull. She is an easy boat to control and very responsive, pointing high and planing quickly. Her cockpit makes for comfortable and dry sailing, and has an easily accessible storage forward. With her simple sloop rig, she's an excellent dinghy for daysailing and racing. With her uncomplicated rig, stability and ease of handling, the **CL 14** is quite suitable for teaching purposes.

Her pivoting mahogany centerboard and rudder blade make it easy to sail in shallow waters and helpful for launching. Some of the **CL 14**'s standard equipment includes hiking straps, boweye, boom-vang and *much* more. To get more of an edge when racing, there's an optional spinnaker available.

Manufacturer: C & L Boatworks, 884 Dillingham Road, Pickering, Ontario, Canada L1W 1Z6. 416/839-7991

SPECIFICATIONS: CL 14
LOA: 14'2", Beam: 5'7", Weight: 240 lbs., Sail Area: 120 s.f., Draft: board up 8", board down 3'6".
Approximate Price: $3495 (Canadian Currency).

MANCHAC

The **MANCHAC DAYSAILER** is a quality, hand-crafted boat that will provide you with years of sailing pleasure. Ron Chapman designed her for sailing on Lake Pontchartrain, one of America's largest inland lakes. She is unique among small sailboats because she comes equipped complete with oars, oarlocks, and bulkhead mounted compass. She is ready for a day cruise.

This 14'4" sloop has a beam of 6'2". The resulting 42% beam ratio adds tremendously to the **MANCHAC's** initial stability, as well as improving her accommodations. She possesses a full entry which affords good buoyancy forward for dry sailing. The full midsection gradually tapers to a classic champagne glass stern, permits an easy turbulence-free exit for displaced water below.

Her interior is very roomy and comfortable with 8' long bench seats and very good leg room. Two compartments lie forward. The first houses a self-draining rope locker complete with anchor and 100' of nylon rope. The second is a sizable storage locker for life jackets, etc.

Rigging and hull construction are excellent quality and positive foam flotation makes her unsinkable. The owner of a **MANCHAC** can take pride in the fact that no corners have been cut in building her.

Manufacturer: Ron Chapman, Shipwright, 324 E. Solidelle, Chalmette, LA 70043. 504/277-6526

SPECIFICATIONS:
MANCHAC
LOA: 14'4", LWL: 12'6", Beam: 6'2", Draft: board up - 6", board down - 33", Displacement: 385 lbs., Sail Area: 106 s.f., Capacity: 4 adults.

Approximate Price: $3600

LASER II

If blistering speed and dynamite performance are what you're looking for in a sailboat, **LASER II** is the boat for you. From the moment that the wind picks up and you step out on the trapeze, **LASER II** is off like a bullet. You feel the boat accelerate below you as the hull leaps onto a plane. The spray is everywhere. The boat, the water, the wind all come together for an exciting ride.

Racing a **LASER II** under full power of 234 s.f. of sail (including spinnaker) on a sailboat that weighs 160 pounds is an experience you'll never forget. The exceptionally stiff hull will respond to your every movement. The oversize and bendy rig will challenge both light and heavy crews. Hull and rig are virtually indestructible.

Both the Canadian Yachting Association and the United States Yacht Racing Union have selected the **LASER II** as their national Youth Championship Training boat. That means you are assured of a top quality, high performance boat for years to come. You will find the **LASER II** easy to learn on and a challenge to master.

One look at a **LASER II** and you'll notice that the cockpit is completely open and roomy so you can move from side to side without injury. The mast is mounted on the deck, out of the way. The hull is tough and rugged to withstand punishment. The control lines are simple and the boat is perfectly balanced for easy sailing. In the event of a capsize, the water empties out completely, so you're off and ready to go quickly and safely.

Class Association: Laser II International Class Association, Fiona Kidd, P.O. Box 569, Hawkesbury, Ontario, Canada K6A 3C8. 613/632-4415
Manufacturer: Laser International, P.O. Box 569, 1250 Tessier St., Hawkesbury, Ontario, Canada K6A 3C8. 613/632-1181

SPECIFICATIONS: LASER II
LOA: 14'5", Beam: 4'8", Hull Weight: 160 lbs., Sail Area: 234 s.f.   **Approximate Price:** $3100

LASER II

DOLPHIN SUPER SENIOR

DOLPHIN SUPER SENIOR has earned the reputation of being one of the world's top-selling sailboats of its class. Its hydro-dynamically correct design, precisely molded in durable fiberglass, well-balanced hull, highly efficient sail and well engineered rigging combine to make this boat a true sailing vessel. She seems to come alive at the slightest breeze.

The **DOLPHIN SUPER SENIOR** has built-in flotation and a self-draining cockpit. She's large enough for two and comes complete with a built-in ice box.

Dolphin has proven itself many times over as a winner in competition, or if you're looking for a craft

DOLPHIN SUPER SENIOR

just for the pleasure and enjoyment that sailing provides, **DOLPHIN SUPER SENIOR** is a very good choice -- so easy to sail, you're an expert in minutes.

Manufacturer: Dolphin Enterprises, Inc., Route 2, Box 111A, Winslow, Arkansas 72959. 501/634-2541

SPECIFICATIONS:
DOLPHIN SUPER
SENIOR
LOA: 14'6"
Beam: 51"
Weight: 170 lbs.
Mast: 11'
Sail Area: 85 s.f.

Approximate
Price: $1825.

MISTRAL 15

Many diligent hours of design engineering have been concentrated on **MISTRAL 15** hull displacement, mast-sail relation, down-haul and sheeting, creating an extremely fast, light and very stable sailboat. The **MISTRAL 15** is a craft designed to delight weekend sailors and experts alike.

Easy to maneuver, it was conceived to provide maximum performance..maximum satisfaction. Light enough for car-top transportation, the **MISTRAL 15** is none the less the perfect solution for a crew of 1 to 3.

Enthusiasts, beginners and experts are still discovering its many advantages.

Manufacturer: Canadian Yacht Builders, P.O. Box 67, Dorion, Quebec, Canada J7V 5V8. 514/455-6183

SPECIFICATIONS:
MISTRAL 15
LOA: 14'8", LWL: 13'6", Beam: 5'0", Draft: Daggerboard up 4", Daggerboard down 3'8", Weight: 145 lbs., Sail Area: 86 s.f.

Approximate Price: $1948

FINN

The **FINN** is a cat-rigged racing machine. First built in 1949, she has been an Olympic boat since 1952. This famous dinghy, designed by Richard Sarby, is the only single-handed dinghy in the Olympics classes.

Her main sheet is three-part and carries a curved traveler. Some of the **FINN**'s gear includes lever boom vang, Cunningham, and aluminum centerboard which is anodized and treated with Teflon.

FINN

For safety, she has three bailers, flotation tanks, and adjustable hiking straps.

Class Association: Finn Class Association, Chip Johns, 79 Joyce St., Warren, RI 02885.

Manufacturer: Vanguard Racing Sailboats, 79 Joyce Street, Warren, RI 02885. 401/245-8608

SPECIFICATIONS: FINN
LOA: 14'9", Beam: 4'10", Wt.: 319 lbs., Draft: board up - 3", board down - 2'3", Weight: 319 lbs., Sail Area: 115 s.f.

Approximate Price: $7800.

AMERICAN 15 DAYSAILOR

This sharp looking 15-footer was introduced in 1986 as a competitor to the International 420 class, as a collegiate or club trainer.

The **AMERICAN 15** was designed for performance, but will also make a fine family daysailer with room for four in her wide, comfortable cockpit. Also featured is roller reefing main, kick-up rudder, compartment for drink cooler, tabernackle mast and optional cuddy cap to cover the open bow.

Priced at under $3000, she's complete and ready to sail with trailer, and can be easily towed behind a small car.

Manufacturer:
American Sail, Inc.
7350 Pepperdam
Avenue, Charleston,
SC 29418.
803/552-8548

SPECIFICATIONS:
AMERICAN 15
DAYSAILOR
LOA: 15'
Width: 5'10"
Hull Weight:
 290 lbs.
Draft:
 Board down 42"
Sail Area: 130 s.f.

Approximate:
Price $2995
(Trailer included).

GYPSY

The **GYPSY** is a "tack and tape" constructed dinghy designed by Phil Bolger. This type construction keeps the cost down and is ideal for the amateur builder. The graceful **GYPSY** will sail, row or motor equally well.

Harold H. "Dynamite" Payson offers the **GYPSY** ready to sail or will sell you plans for $30.00. Home building cost is approximately $500 (including sail). Harold also has available approximately 20 other plans (designs available) and offers a catalogue of study plans for $3.00.

Manufacturer: Harold H. Payson, Pleasant Beach Road, So. Thomaston, ME 04858. 207/594-7587

SPECIFICATIONS: **GYPSY**
LOA: 15', Beam: 4', Weight: 400 lbs.

Approximate Price: $1500.

MERCURY SLOOP

Some 2000 **MERCURY SLOOPS** were built of wood between 1940 and 1952. At that time, the **MERCURY** was considered by many to be the best all-around small boat on the market, so investment was made in a fiberglass mold. The first ten boats went to the Community Boating Program on the Charles River in Boston, where they are still giving good service in a fleet now numbering more than 80 **MERCURYS**.

The Class has grown steadily and the Mercury Class Association has fleets actively sailing from Maine to Florida, with a large number of fleets in the Greater Boston Area. This exceptional sailboat is also used widely

MERCURY SLOOP

for instruction and enjoyment at many camps, such as Camp Alton, Camp Avalon, Cape Cod SeaCamps, Camp Belknap, Camp Viking.

The **MERCURY SLOOP** has the balance one would expect from a Sparkman & Stephen's design, and is as fast or faster than most other non-planing boats; stable enough for beginners and lively enough to hold the interest of experienced adults with Genoa and spinnakers as options.

As in other Cape Cod boats, you can depend on the sturdy construction and fine appearance of this boat. Her fittings are of the highest grade, assuring dependability. Her teak splashboards enhance her beauty, and the two air flotation tanks in her fiberglass seats insure safety. These are just a few reasons why the **MERCURY** is such an appealing sailboat.

The **MERCURY** is available as either a keel or a centerboard boat with the price the same for both. Select a model to fit your local water conditions.

Manufacturer: Cape Cod Shipbuilding Co., Wareham, MA 02571. 617/295-3550

SPECIFICATIONS: MERCURY SLOOP
LOA: 15', LWL: 13'10", Beam: 5'5", Draft: C/B - 39", Keel 29", Weight: Keel - 730 lbs., C/B - 470 lbs., Sail Area: 119 s.f.

Approximate Price: $5408

MINUTEMAN

A broad, stable hull, a large main on a traditional gaff rig, high bow and coamings. MINUTEMAN's relationships to an ordinary catboat ends there. She is a one-design cat, designed to be quick (she'll outpoint a sloop), while retaining the safe, seaworthy characteristics that make catboating a great way to daysail.

If you're planning to enter a club race, you'll take pride in MINUTEMAN's performance. If a leisurely afternoon's sail is more to your liking, her 10-foot cockpit is a great place to relax with a friend or two or even solo.

MINUTEMAN is sturdily built with a hand laid up hull, heavy duty mast primed and painted, positive foam flotation between interior liner and hull. The red boot top and a self-bailing cockpit are standard. And she's traditionally outfitted. Teak trim, oak mast hoops, bronze hardware and a flag insignia sail give MINUTEMAN a stylish, classic cat appearance.

A cuddy cabin is standard at no extra cost. Her own trailer is the only thing you would need to add to take MINUTEMAN sailing anywhere.

Manufacturer:
Nauset Marine, Inc.
Route 6A,
Orleans, MA 02653
617/255-0777

SPECIFICATIONS:
MINUTEMAN
LOA: 15', LWL: 14'7",
Beam: 6'6", Draft:
board up 8", board
down 3'9", Displacement: 800 lbs., Sail
Area: 145 s.f.

**Approximate
Price:** $6200

MINUTEMAN

ISLANDS 15

The all new **ISLANDS 15** is a remarkable design for open water, bay or lake sailing. She is easy to rig and easy to sail, even single-handedly, but will accommodate six adults comfortable in her roomy cockpit. She is fast and planes with ease, but is also stiff and forgiving even to novice sailors. The broad beam provides the **ISLANDS 15** with great stability and safety. The gunwales are flared for maximum dryness and rigidity. Large dry below deck storage is provided under the foredeck and optional gear compartments are on the port and starboard sides. The boat is self bailing, constructed of hand-laid fiberglass and features a complete liner and extra roomy decks with integral non-skid surfaces. Molded in place foam makes the boat unsinkable.

The centerboard is completely enclosed and is constructed of fiberglass, with a purchase lift of 2:1. The kick-up rudder of 3/16" aluminum is pivot-mounted between marine plywood cheeks, which is fitted with stainless steel hardware, a wood tiller and tiller extension.

Spars are made of anodized aluminum, and include spinnaker hardware, vang bails, downhaul, outhaul and halyard cleats. The mast step is hinged for fast and easy mast placement and can be taken down by one sailor. Standing rigging is stainless; the forestay turnbuckle, shroud adjusters, chainplates and travel rod are all stainless steel. All blocks are top quality. The main and jib halyards are braided Dacron, and sails are of quality DuPont Dacron.

Manufacturer: Sumner Boat Company, Inc., 334 S. Bayview Avenue, Amityville, NY 11701. 516/264-1830

SPECIFICATIONS: ISLANDS 15'
LOA: 15'3", LWL: 13'6", Beam: 6'6.5", Draft: board up 6", board down 3'6", Sail Area: Main 81.5 s.f., Jib 39.5 s.f., Weight: 420 lbs., Bridge Clearance: 22'1"

Approximate Price: $3095

ISLANDS 15

CORONADO 15

The **CORONADO 15** is a high performance, strict one-design centerboarder that doubles as an exciting racing sloop and a comfortable family daysailer. Her speed is exceptional. She planes easily and is extremely responsive to all points of wind. A trapeze is available for added ease in handling. The boat has been selected by many collegiate sailing teams and the military for world wide use.

With a large completely self-bailing cockpit, the **CORONADO 15** has storage in the foredeck for sailing gear and personal belongings. Two wide foam-filled tanks provide comfort, positive flotation and allows the boat to be self-rescued easily.

She is constructed of 100% hand-lay fiberglass for the ultimate in strength and ease in maintenance. Spars are of anodized aluminum and easy to maintain. All hulls are white with molded-in waterlines, and there is a large selection of colored non-skid and colored decks.

Manufacturer: Capri Sailboats, 21200 Victory Boulevard, Woodland Hills, California 91367. 818/884-7700

Class Association: Coronado 15 Class Racing Association, 1117 North Formosa Avenue, Los Angeles, CA 90046.

SPECIFICATIONS:
CORONADO 15
LOA: 15'4"
Beam: 5'8"
Weight" 385 lbs.
Sail Area: 139 s.f.

Approximate Price: $2550

CORONADO 15

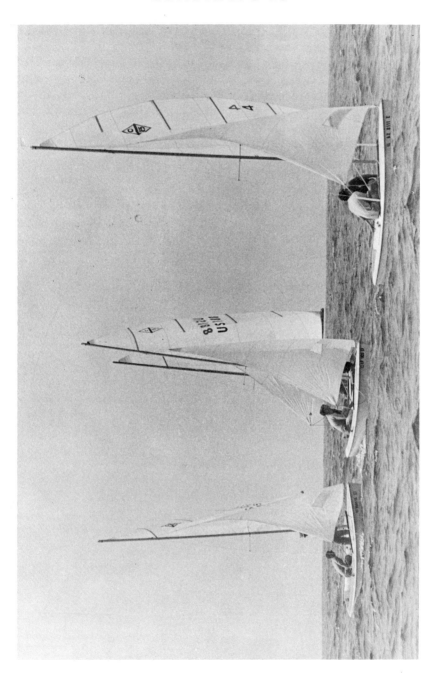

INTERNATIONAL 470

The **470 CLASS** is the world's biggest high performance racing dinghy class -- over 30,000 sail numbers -- it is truly International, which is why it was chosen for the Olympic Games. In 1976, she became an Olympic class and more recently was selected as the boat to be used in the new women's Olympic sailing event at the 1988 Olympic Games. While providing the thrills and high level of competition expected of an Olympic Class, it is suited for both light weights and family racing.

For Club racing, the **470's** successful handicap performance guarantees popularity and the active National Class Association ensures a wide choice of open meetings and a class administration, which is assisting the build-up of new fleets and the future of the Class.

Class Association: United States 470 Association, Rick Stevenson, President, 2202 Arborview Drive, Maryland Heights, Missouri 63043.

Manufacturer: Vanguard Racing Sailboats, 79 Joyce St. Warren, RI 02885. 401/245-8608

Manufacturer's Rep: International Sailing Products, Inc., P.O. Box 355, Oyster Bay, New York 11771. 516/922-5182.

SPECIFICATIONS:
INTERNATIONAL 470
LOA: 15'5"
Beam: 5'6"
Weight: 268 lbs.
Sail Area:
 Main & Jib 137 s.f.
 Spinnaker 140 s.f.

Approximate
Price: $7000.

INTERNATIONAL 470

MISTRAL 4.7

The **MISTRAL 4.7** is the "total" competitive sailboat. The structural ingenuity of the **MISTRAL 4.7**, a modern unique, sloop design, is its claim to being the sailboat built by experts, for experts.

The **MISTRAL 4.7** is one of the most outstanding craft you could wish to own. Everything about it says speed, reliability and performance.

Some of her standard equipment includes hiking straps, hiking strap cushions, adjustable cunningham, stainless steel rigging, fiberglass centerboard and kick-up rudder, tiller extension, boom vang, spinnaker rigging, trapeze system, and much more.

Optional equipment available includes spinnaker and pole, trapeze belt, wind indicator and masthead float.

MISTRAL 4.7

A sporty, aggressive craft capable of high speeds, the MISTRAL 4.7 is a sailboat for sportsmen and competitive sailors.

Manufacturer: Canadian Yacht Builders, P.O. Box 67, Dorion, Quebec, Canada   J7V 5V8.   514/455-6183

PECIFICATIONS: MISTRAL 4.7
OA: 15'5", LWL: 13'10", Beam: 5'2", Draft: Centerboard up ", Centerboard down 3'2", Weight: 255 lbs., Sail Area: 1ain 89 s.f., Jib 56 s.f., Spinnaker 175 s.f.

pproximate Price: $3450

SANDPIPER

This shoal-draft catboat's ancestry goes back to the late 1800's in the area south of Cape Cod. Strong winds, heavy currents and shoals demand a tough, fast and easy to handle boat, while carrying a large payload.

Breck Marshall designed the **SANDPIPER** in 1972 after years of producing the famous **Sanderling**. Fiberglass construction allows for more efficient sailing and less maintenance.

This beautiful, easy to operate, stable catboat makes a great family daysailer or fleet racer. This classic will also turn heads. She is offered in both open and cuddy models.

Manufacturer: Marshall Marine Corp., Shipyard Lane, P.O. Box P-266, S. Dartmouth, MA 02748. 617/994-0414

SPECIFICATIONS:
SANDPIPER
LOA: 15'6"
Beam: 7'1"
Draft:
 board up 16"
 board down 3'9"
Sail Area: 166 s.f.
Displacement:
 1050 lbs.
Ballast: 200 lbs.

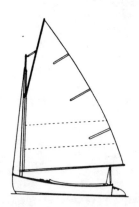

Approximate
Price: $7100

O most merciful Lord, we beseech Thee for courage in the time of fear, wisdom when human knowledge runs out, enthusiastic interest when life becomes drab and always a sense of Thy presence with us. Be very near unto any of our shipmates who are tempted to lose heart and faith. Amen.

SANDPIPER

Photo by: Norman Fortier

SNIPE

The **SNIPE** is sailed throughout the world. Over 27,000 have been built, and there are 800 chartered Snipe Fleets. This International Class appeals to all ages and boasts of three-generation **SNIPE** families.

Here is a boat that is fast, rugged and fun to sail. From the beginning of its history, the basic lines have not changed, but construction has improved with new materials. She's a good looking and roomy daysailer.

SNIPE Class Association is large and well organized, with a full-time office and monthly publication. **SNIPE** sailors are fun to be with. The Class attracts the world's top sailors.

This boat is not expensive and, because of its popularity, there are many used boats available also.

Class Association: Snipe Class International Racing Association, Inc., Privateer Road, Hixson Tennessee 37343.

Manufacturer: Alax Yachts, S.W. Camet, P.O. Box 83599, San Diego, CA 92138. 619/224-6737
Manufacturer: McLaughlin Boat Works, 4737 Adams Road, Hixson, TN 37343. 615/875-4040

SPECIFICATIONS:
SNIPE
LOA: 15'6"
LWL: 13'6"
Beam: 5'
Sail Area: 128 s.f.
Draft:
 board up 6"
 board down 3'3"
Minimum Weight:
 381 lbs.
Approximate
Price: $4800

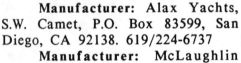

SNIPE

Photo by: Buzz Lamb

WINDMILL

The **WINDMILL** was conceived in Clearwater, Florida, in the early 1950's by Clark Mills, who also designed the famous **Optimist** in 1947. The boat was designed to provide the amateur builder means to inexpensively move from the pram to a more high performance daysailer. Mr. Mills certainly accomplished his goal. Over 5000 have been registered since 1953, and she twice won the One-Of-A-Kind invitational regatta.

For the do-it-yourselfer, the **WINDMILL** can be built in about two months, or it can be purchased in fiberglass.

This high performance machine will plane in ten knots of wind. Some feel it is the fastest one-design that can be built by the amateur, and it may be the fastest one-design for the money. She is sailed without trapeze or spinnaker, which keeps it simple for the family sailor.

This is a well organized class, which has fleets in many states. If you are looking for a hot boat at a low cost, contact the association.

Class Association: Windmill Class Association, P.O Box 43564, Birmingham, Alabama 35243.

Manufacturer: McLaughlin Boat Works, 4737 Adams Road, Hixson, TN 37343. 615/875-4040

SPECIFICATIONS: WINDMILL
LOA: 15'6", Beam: 4'8", Sail Area: 119 s.f., Hull Weight 198 lbs., Draft: centerboard up - 6", centerboard down 4'2", Mast Height: 20'3".

Approximate Price:
Ready-made in fiberglass - $3600.
Cost to build and rig in wood - $1500 to $1800.

WINDMILL

CAROLINA CATBOAT

The **CATBOAT** is recognized as one of the true American boats with a history that can be traced to the Colonial era. Around Cape Cod, strong winds, tides and treacherous shoals demanded a design that would stand up to all sailing conditions and function as a work boat, cruising boat, daysailer, and racing boat. The boats had to be shoal draft, fast, seaworthy, weatherly, handy, and comfortable. The solution that evolved was the catboat. The **CAROLINA CAT** combines the traditional design with modern building techniques and a simple, easily handled rig creating a boat that's a joy to sail.

With her wide beam, the **CATBOAT** has remarkable stability and tremendous reserve buoyancy in proportion to her displacement. This allows her to rise quickly to oncoming seas and keep her decks dry in the process.

Sailing when the breeze is up, or ghosting along in light air, the **CAROLINA CAT** will amaze you with her big boat feel, yet she is responsive to the lightest touch on the tiller. She comes about with a smooth, positive motion which is a handy feature for close-quarters sailing.

Like many of her forerunners, the **CAROLINA CAT** has an unstayed mast which is easily stepped and rigged so that you can get underway in a matter of minutes. The gaff rig is simple to set up and there is only one sheet to handle. Spars are stored in the boat when not in use.

The huge cockpit is a great place to stretch out and relax. Laminated mahogany coamings look great and provide a comfortable back rest. The seats are 7' long and wide enough to sleep on. With optional dodger and roll-up side curtains, an instant cabin is ready for an overnight stay at some quiet anchorage.

You can gunkhole to your heart's content with her 10-inch draft or beach her for a picnic somewhere off the beaten path.

CAROLINA CATBOAT

Manufacturer: N.L. Silva & Co., 7980 Market St., Wilmington, NC 28405. 919/686-4356

SPECIFICATIONS: CAROLINA CAT
LOA: 15'8", Beam: 7'4", Draft: board up - 10", board down - 3'; Sail Area: 151 s.f., Displacement: 1600 lbs., Capacity: 6+ adults.

Approximate Price: $7500.

POINT JUDE

The **POINT JUDE** was designed in 1948, and was manufactured for twenty years as a wooden boat. During the transition to fiberglass, several design changes have been made, but for the last four years, this classical good looking daysailer has been made to strict one-design standards.

The hard chine and high freeboard make it a stable, dry boat to sail. Her twin 7' bench seats and 25 cubic feet of lockable storage make **POINT JUDE** a very comfortable boat for family daysailing.

POINT JUDE

Over 500 **POINT JUDES** are presently sailing in the northeastern U.S. Her look is richly traditional...teak trim, green hull, tan-bark sails, etc. She's a beautiful boat in the water. Sea-kindly and built to last, this is an ideal family daysailer.

Manufacturer: Starwing, Inc., P.O. Box 137, Bristol, RI 02809. 401/254-0670

SPECIFICATIONS:
POINT JUDE
LOA: 15'8"
Beam: 5'11"
Draft:
 board up 8"
 board down 3'4"
Weight: 525 lbs.
Sail Area: 136 s.f.

Approximate
Price: $4500.

For New Year's Day

O Thou who art from everlasting to everlasting, in whose sight a thousand years are but as a day, replenish us with Thy spirit, that we may take hope as we face this New Year. Thou art merciful and will forgive seventy times seven. Thou hast given us a new log. Help us to make such entries from day to day which will be pleasing in Thy sight. Suffer not the coming days to separate us from Thee. Amen.

BULL'S-EYE

Cape Cod Shipbuilding has been producing the fiberglass **BULL'S-EYE** since 1948. The hull is essentially the same as the **H-12** or **Doughdish** or other named Herreshoff 12-footers (see these for the history of this design). The major difference is the more modern marconi rig and cuddy cabin.

When it comes to rough water, this is one of the most stable daysailers available. She has a full keel containing 750 lbs. of lead. This is also a roomy, comfortable boat for the size. She carries a full sailing rig, including genoa or spinnaker.

The class association is quite large, with fleets concentrated on the east coast. If you like the stability and look of a time-proven hull design, but want a more modern sail rig, check out the Cape Cod **BULL'S-EYE**.

Class Association: Bull's Eye Class Association, 37 Atlantic Avenue, Rockport, MA 01966.

Manufacturer: Cape Cod Shipbuilding Co., Narrows Road, Box 152, Wareham, Massachusetts 02571. 617/295-3550

SPECIFICATIONS:
BULL'S-EYE
LOA: 15' 8.5"
LWL: 12' 6.75"
Beam: 5'10"
Draft: 2'5"
Weight: 1350 lbs.
Sail Area: 140 s.f.

Approximate
Price: $7837

BULL'S-EYE

H-12

Captain Nathaniel Herreshoff designed and produced the original in 1914. The **H-12** of that day was called **Bull's Eye**. Actually, she has been called many different names during the years, such as **Doughdish, Bristol Class, H-Class,** and other local names. Whatever name you use, this is one of the most famous daysailers.

The **H-12** was designed to handle the rough waters in Buzzards Bay. This same hull design is used on the present day **Doughdish** and the Cape Cod **Bull's Eye** and has lasted for over 70 years. This long life didn't just happen.

The **H-12** is Cape Cod Shipbuilding's fiberglass recreation of the original Herreshoff design. The hull shape is basically the same. The interior may have changed slightly, but she has retained that old charm. The **H-12** name comes from her waterline length, which was the custom in older times, even though her overall length is more than 15 feet.

The gaff rig and spruce spars may seem strange at first, but it doesn't take long to realize why this rig has been used for centuries.

If you're interested in a classic beauty for your next daysailer, be sure to include the **H-12** on your shopping list.

Manufacturer: Cape Cod Shipbuilding Co., Wareham, Massachusetts 02571. 617/295-3550

SPECIFICATIONS: H-12
LOA: 15'8.5"
LWL: 12'6"
Beam: 5'10"
Draft: 29"
Displacement: 1350 lbs.
Sail Area: 140 s.f.
Ballast: 750 lbs. lead
Approximate Price: $11,867

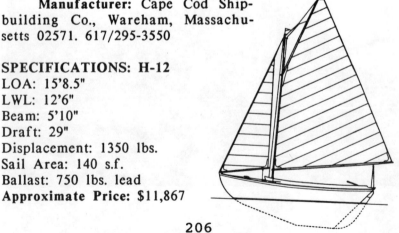

DOUGHDISH

This is another re-creation of the famous Herreshoff 12 1/2 footer (water line length). **Doughdish, Inc.** has chosen one of the more affectionate of the many names used for this great design since the original was produced in 1914.

This reproduction is beautiful and retains the character of the old classics using modern, easily maintained fiberglass hulls. Just about all wood is teak, except for the spruce spars. Great care has been taken to retain the handling characteristics also. She has been incorporated into the original class association.

The **DOUGHDISH** is a great handling daysailer. She is very stable and can be sailed single-handed. She will also sail the entire family in comfort and safety.

The originals were gaff-rigged. In the 1920's, the Marconi rig became popular and has been produced with either rig since, dictated by area more than anything else. These boats are sloop rigged, with self-tending jibs.

Over the years, these boats have been called many names, including **Bull's Eye, Buzzard Bay, Doughdish** and others. It is said the name "**Doughdish**" originated because of its resemblance to the round bottomed dough dish in which bread dough was left to rise.

The class association has 350-360 members, and there are probably several hundred more of these fine boats around the country. The class is growing and, at age 73, is gaining popularity.

If you're looking for a beautiful, time tested daysailer that will perform well, even in rough weather, check out the **DOUGHDISH**.

Manufacturer: Doughdish, Inc., Marion, Massachusetts 02738. 617/748-0334
Manufacturer: Edey & Duff, Ltd., 128 Aucoot Road, Mattapoisett, MA 02739. 617/758-2743

DOUGHDISH

Class Association: "H" Class Association, William G. Harding, Secretary, Box 1, Cataumet, MA 02534

SPECIFICATIONS: DOUGHDISH
LOA: 15'10", LWL: 12'6", Beam: 5'10", Draft: 2'6", Weight: 1500 lbs., Sail Area: 140 s.f.   **Approximate Price: $12,000.**

WAYFARER

This good looking, spirited, roomy daysailer is a great choice for the family. The **WAYFARER** is a boat that can be raced by two or loaded up with the whole family. It can be raced with the standard rig or equipped with a spinnaker for the more serious racer.

The **WAYFARER's** double chine and wide beam make her a very stable planing daysailer. Reports of her crossing the North Sea and Scotland to Iceland passages

WAYFARER

demonstrates her sea-worthiness. Two can sleep on the wide, flat floor and use the boom as a tent support for camping.

Class Association: U.S. Wayfarer Class Association, 2006 Gladwick Street, Compton, CA 90220.

Manufacturer: Abbott Boats, Inc., 1458 London Road, Sarnia, Ontario, N7S 1P7. 519/542-2771

SPECIFICATIONS:
WAYFARER
LOA: 15'10"
LWL: 14'10"
Beam: 6'1"
Draft:
 board up 8"
 board down 3'10"
Weight: 365 lbs.
Sail Area:
 Main 95 s.f.
 Genoa 46 s.f.
 Spinnaker 195 s.f.

Approximate Price: $3700

For Our Motion Picture Operators

Almighty God, we thank Thee for the services of our motion picture operators. We realize that often when we can go ashore on liberty, they have to stay aboard. For all who strive to make our duty pleasant on this ship, we give Thee thanks. We are mindful of our needs. Keep us from being molded, in our weakness, by the world but let our strength so shape events that Thy Kingdom will hasten. Amen.

DINGHIES AND DAYSAILERS /
16' To 19.99'

CL 16

The dependable **CL 16** is a sloop rigged dinghy designed for safe, comfortable daysailing and cruising. She can accommodate six passengers for fun daysailing, or can be easily be sailed by a crew of two for racing.

With her graceful, double chined planing hull, the **CL 16** behaves quite well in almost any weather conditions. She provides speed and maneuverability in light air, plus stability and safety in heavy weather.

Like all of the boats from C & L Boatworks, she has a pivoting mahogany rudder blade and centerboard. She's also equipped with hiking straps, boom-vang and teak side benches. The **CL 16** is a fun and *fast* boat.

Manufacturer: C & L Boatworks, 884 Dillingham Road, Pickering, Ontario, Canada L1W 1Z6. 416/839-7991

SPECIFICATIONS: CL 16
LOA: 16', LWL: 14'10", Beam: 6'1", Sail Area: main - 95 s.f., genoa - 46 s.f., Draft: centerboard up - 8", centerboard down - 3'10", Weight: 365 lbs.

Approximate Price: $4895 (Canadian Currency).

CLASS X

Realizing the necessity for a safe junior trainer, the Inland Lake Yachting Association adopted the **CLASS X** in 1934. She is the only non-scow governed by the ILYA.

The "X" is a hard-chined, pointed bow, centerboard boat that was designed primarily as a safe and uncomplicated trainer for beginning sailors and racers.

Over the years, this same basic design has provided thousands of sailors with their start in the sport, and it continues to be the predominant racer in the Midwest exclusively for girls and boys up to 16 years of age.

216

CLASS X

Class Association: Inland Lake Yachting Association, P.O. Box 311, Fontana, WI 53125. 414/275-6921

Manufacturer: Melges Boat Works, Zenda, WI 53195. 414/248-6621

Manufacturer: Johnson Boat Works, 4495 Lake Avenue, White Bear Lake, MN 55110. 612/429-7221

SPECIFICATIONS:
CLASS X
LOA: 16'
Beam: 6'1"
Sail Area:
 Main 85 s.f.
 Jib 24.75 s.f.
Weight: 500 lbs.

Approx. Price:
$3989-$4280

Prayer for One Lost Overboard

O Eternal God, who alone spreadest out the heavens, and rulest the raging of the sea; hear our prayers in the behalf of him who is lost overboard. If it is Thy will that he be not found then grant him an entrance into the land of light and glory. Bless those who mourn his passing and uphold them with Thy mercy and strength. Be Thou our stay in this time of trial and our hope for all our days. Grant unto us, his shipmates, such faith and hope, that when we shall depart this life, we may receive the kingdom prepared for us, from the beginning of the world, through Christ our Lord. Amen.

INTERNATIONAL CONTENDER

The **INTERNATIONAL CONTENDER** is a single-handed trapeze boat, sporting the sail area of a **Finn**, on a longer and more easily driven planing hull. Designed in 1968 by Bob Miller of **Australia II** fame, **CONTENDER** was granted International status by the International Yacht Racing Union (IYRU) in 1969, as an alternate to the **Finn**. Since that time, the number of boats has grown steadily: IYRU reports 56 new **CONTENDERS** registered in 1986.

While this exciting single-hander has been traditionally dominated by the Europeans, recent events have turned this around: the World Champion for 1984 and 1985 was Australian, and the World Champion for 1986 was from the USA. The continued promise is for exciting international racing, not dominated by a single person or country, where victory goes to the shrewdest helmsman, not the biggest spender. And old boats don't die: the top five finishers at the 1986 Worlds sailed chartered boats, the youngest of which was three years old.

The **CONTENDER** is typically built of GRP hull, either foam or baba cored, with glass or wood deck. However, there are wood kits available. Deck layouts vary wildly, with most people opting for simplicity, the reason being that you can't sail fast with your head on the cockpit tweaking controls. The Class strictly controls the structure of the hull, while leaving the rest up to the individual.

The performance of the **CONTENDER** is unparalleled amongst single-handers. In breezes over 8 knots, this boat will plane on a reach; and, in breezes over 12 knots, she'll plane to weather. The helmsman must keep the boat in trim fore and aft, as well as side to side from the wire. This activity has been compared to a foot race. But best of all, the **CONTENDER** is **fun**; after a day's worth of explosive acceleration and sheets of spray, who cannot come home with a smile on their lips?!

INTERNATIONAL CONTENDER

There are currently active fleets in Northern and Southern California, Ohio, Texas and Maryland, and other areas are seeing budding interest in this thoroughbred.

Class Association: International Contender Class Association, Charles Wright, 214 N. Winnetka Ave., Dallas, TX 75208.

SPECIFICATIONS: CONTENDER
LOA: 16', Beam: 4'8", Draft: board up 5", board down 4', Hull Weight: 185 lbs., Rigged Weight: 228 lbs., Sail Area: 120 s.f.
Approximate Price: $3500 - $5000.

JOHNSON J SAILER

It's tough to talk about the **J SAILER** without resorting to superlatives. You'll understand the first time you take her out for a solo sail in a good wind.

She sails outstandingly well in a heavy blow or a light breeze. The simple, but sufficient rigging, make it very easy for the beginner to sail, as well as provide the experienced sailor with all he needs to *push it to the limit*.

The **JOHNSON J SAILER** is an extremely well-built boat with the very best equipment, like large bailers and Harken ball bearing pulleys. She will provide the new sailor or the expert with many years of enjoyable sailing.

JOHNSON J SAILER

Manufacturer: Johnson Boat Works, 4495 Lake Avenue, White Bear Lake, MN 55110. 612/429-7221

SPECIFICATIONS:
JOHNSON J SAILER
LOA: 16'
Beam: 5'8"
Sail Area: 123 s.f.
Draft: 3'
Capacity: 1-4 persons

Approximate
Price: $3950

LEEWARD 16

This do-it-yourself kit boat has been in production over twenty years and thousands have been built. The basic kit can be assembled in one week-end.

LEEWARD's wide, semi-planing hull is exceptionally stable and roomy. Her cockpit will seat six on chair-high molded-in seats with form fitting backrests. Cockpit seats and all decks have molded-in non-skid surfaces. All lines are located conveniently for single-handed sailing. Centerboard and rudder can tip up or retract fully for beaching.

Luger Boats offers options for the **LEEWARD** like a special trailer, Genoa, motor mount, cover, etc. to complete this sturdy daysailer.

Manufacturer:
Luger Boats, 424 South 8th. Street, St. Joseph, MO 64502
816/233-5116

SPECIFICATIONS:
LEEWARD 16
LOA: 16'
Beam: 6'3"
Draft:
 board up 4"
 board down 45"
Weight: 650 lbs.
Sail Area: 140 s.f.

Approximate Price: $2500

WHITEHALL 16

The 16' WHITEHALL has overall dimensions proportionate to the original 12-footer, but Harry Sylvester added twin daggerboards for sailing. This was done in order to maintain the center rowing position. The WHITEHALL 16 can be used as a large rowing boat with three rowing positions, or as a traditional sailboat with gaff main and jib. The wineglass stern, graceful sheer and sharp entry all add to the classic beauty of this design.

Like all of the B&S WHITEHALLS, materials are of top quality; mahogany seats and gunnels, completely hand laid up fiberglass hull, bronze hardware, and more.

Manufacturer: B&S Corp., Harrison C. Sylvester, Bessey Ridge Road, Albion Maine 04910. 207/437-9245

SPECIFICATIONS: WHITEHALL 16
LOA: 16', Weight: 200 lbs., Sail Area: Main 78 s.f., Jib 33 s.f., Draft: 26".

Approx. Price: Sprit - $2945, Gaff - $3745, Row - $1845.

M-16 SCOW

This sporty 16-footer is the perfect scow for two moderately sized people weighing a total of 240-310 lbs. to race or pleasure sail. Typically, this includes combinations of husband and wife, parent and child, brothers and sisters, and graduates from the junior racing programs - as well as other adults. The boat has all the sail-handling adjustments necessary for a modern sloop and a true scow hull design that makes her very fast and lively. She is easy to sail and not complicated with spinnaker gear, making the crew-work less demanding than on other boats.

The **M-16 SCOW** was developed in the late 1950's and is one of the classes represented by the Inland Lake Yachting Association, which is approximately 4000 strong. This is one of the best organized class associations, which provides good competition and comraderie.

M-16 SCOW

Class Association: Inland Lake Yachting Association, P.O. Box 311, Fontana, WI 53125. 414/275-6921

Manufacturer: Melges Boat Works, Zenda, WI 53195. 414/248-6621

Manufacturer: Johnson Boat Works, 4495 Lake Avenue, White Bear Lake, MN 55110. 612/429-7221

Manufacturer: Bowland Boat Works, Box 585, Bobcaygeon, Ontario, Canada K0M 1A0. 705/738-3613

SPECIFICATIONS:
M-16 SCOW
LOA: 16'
Beam: 5'8"
Sail Area: 147 s.f.
Weight: 440 lbs.

Approximate
Price: $6169-$6500

The Navy Prayer

"O Eternal Lord God, who alone spreadest out the heavens and rulest the raging of the sea; vouchsafe to take into Thy almighty and most gracious protection our country's Navy and all who serve therein. Preserve them from the dangers of the sea and from the violence of the enemy; that they may be a safeguard unto the United States of America and a security for such as pass on the seas upon their lawful occasions; that the inhabitants of our land may in peace and quietness serve Thee our God to the glory of Thy name; through Jesus Christ our Lord. Amen.

MC SCOW

This is the newest of the Inland Lakes Yachting Association's scows. The **MC** is also a National Class boat, which should appeal to the larger single-handed racing sailor or a crew of two lighter-weight racers. This smaller scow might also appeal to anyone looking for a responsive daysailer/racer to be used by the entire family.

Although this simple cat-rigged beauty can be sailed by almost any sailor, the **MC SCOW** can test the skills of the very experienced racer when sailed to its maximum potential.

Class Association: Inland Lake Yachting Association P.O. Box 311, Fontana, WI 53125. 414/275-6921

Class Association: International MC Class Sailboat Racing Association, 3213 Shore Rd., Ft. Collins, CO 80524 303/484-6293

MC SCOW

Manufacturer: Melges Boat Works, Zenda, WI 53195. 414/248-6621

Manufacturer: Johnson Boat Works, 4495 Lake Ave., White Bear Lake, MN 55110. 612/429-7221

SPECIFICATIONS:
MC SCOW
LOA: 16'
Beam: 5'8"
Sail Area: 135 s.f.
Hull Wt.: 420 lbs.

Approx. Price:
$4972-$5300

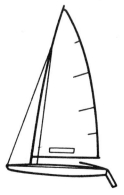

227

MISTRAL 16

The **MISTRAL 16** is a surprising sailboat; its prove
double chine hull design enhances rapid acceleration a
the slightest breeze, in comfort and safety.

Its competitive power lies well hidden beneath
discreet outer styling. But as the wind rises, th
MISTRAL 16 awakes, leaps and planes across the wate
with astonishing speed and ease.

The **MISTRAL 16**, in a class of its own, accommo
dating a crew of up to six persons, will amaze you wit
its extremely well appointed cockpit and conveniences
surpassed only by sailing performance.

The **MISTRAL 16**, designed by sailors, for sailors, i
the sailboat which answers the most demanding require
ments of family and competition sailing.

Manufacturer: Canadian Yacht Builders, P.O. Box 67
Dorion Quebec, Canada J7V 5V8. 514/455-6183

MISTRAL 16

SPECIFICATIONS: MISTRAL 16

LOA: 16', LWL: 14'10", Beam: 6'1", Draft: Centerboard up ", Centerboard down 3'10", Weight: 365 lbs., Sail Area: Main 95 s.f., Jib 46 s.f., Spinnaker 195 s.f.

Approximate Price: $3790.

NORSKA

In Norway, this type of boat is called a Hardangersjekte. The name comes from Hardangersfjord, the place where the design originated. The "jekte" ending of the name means boat. The **NORSKA** is a double-ender, a genuine Norseman, which has all the characteristics of the long ships of the Vikings. In their homeland, the Hardangersjektes were used primarily for fishing, venturing at times many miles offshore in search of suitable catches.

The hull of **NORSKA** is hand laid of glass fibers and polyester resin. The gunwales are "sandwich" construction made of mahogany wood. The rudder, tiller thwarts and interior finishing are of solid mahogany Flotation is provided by two large compartments molded

NORSKA

into the hull with a well for a small outboard motor molded into the aft compartment. She comes with either a weighted keel or aluminum daggerboard. The mast is secured by both a mast step and partner as well as a forestay and pair of shrouds. Spars are anodized aluminum (wood spars are available). The sail is a spritsail rig consisting of Dacron main and jib available in tanbark or white. All the hardware is stainless steel or brass.

Manufacturer: The PBJ Dory Company, 2024 Pacific Avenue, San Pedro, CA 90731. 213/519-8440

SPECIFICATIONS:
NORSKA
LOA: 16'
Beam: 6'
Sail Area: 98 s.f.

Approximate
Price: $2750.

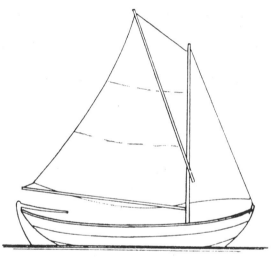

For Our Messmen

Our Father, we thank Thee for daily routine blessings. We would pray for our cooks and messmen who work in the dark hours of the early morning that we may be nourished in body. Keep with us a sense of appreciation for the labors of others. Give unto them a sense of self-satisfaction in their endeavors to provide worthy tables before us from day to day. Amen.

GEMINI

This traditional looking daysailer has something very different below - twin boards. The **GEMINI** has a board installed on each side that protrudes at an angle away from the centerline. The people at Cape Cod Shipbuilding have done a lot of testing and found the boat is much faster with twin boards. When sailing, you simply raise the weather board and lower the leeward board for most efficient speed. Each board is much smaller than single board design. The cockpit is very roomy without the centerboard also.

The **GEMINI** is a well designed, sharp looking, quality built daysailer. She trailers well at only 440 pounds, and her hardware and rigging are high quality. The fractional rig is simple and efficient.

Manufacturer: Cape Cod Shipbuilding Co., Wareham, Massachusetts 02571. 617/295-3550

SPECIFICATIONS:
GEMINI
LOA: 16'1"
LWL: 14'9"
Beam: 5'7"
Draft:
 hull 7"
 boards down 40"
Sail Area: 140 s.f.
Weight: 440 lbs.

Approximate
Price: $5,321.

GEMINI

FIREBALL

The **FIREBALL** was designed in 1963 in England, by Peter Milne. She gained international status by the IYRU in 1970. This hot racing dinghy association has issued over 14,000 sail numbers.

She is a pure racing machine to be used in inland waters. Whatever material you choose, wood or fiberglass, she is light and fast, and a trapeze is needed to keep her upright. She portrays finesse and agility, rather than gorilla strength. Crew weight must be used efficiently when the breeze is up, due to her rather narrow beam.

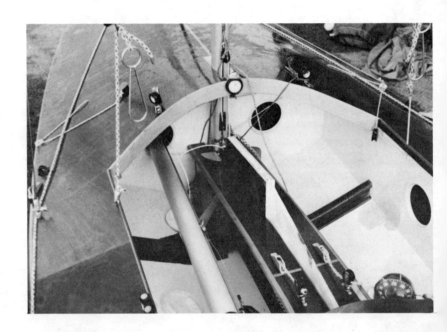

This is an exciting boat to sail. So climb aboard, sheet in and blast off in the boat whose name says it all -- FIREBALL!!

Manufacturer: Outer Limits Yachts, 1073 Summit Avenue, Cleveland, Ohio 44107. 216/221-3846

FIREBALL

Class Association: US International Fireball Association, Chuck Hooker, P.O. Box 39509, Charleston, SC 29407. 803/795-9048

SPECIFICATIONS:
FIREBALL
LOA: 16'2"
Beam: 4' 8.5"
Weight: 175 lbs.
Draft:
 board up 6.5"
 board down 4'.5"
Sail Area:
 Main & Jib 123 s.f.
 Spinnaker 140 s.f.

Approximate Price:
$5500 - $7000.

235

PRECISION 16

This Steve Seaton design is an exceptionally stable, family oriented daysailer that does not sacrifice modern state of the art performance.

The **PRECISION 16**'s generous beam and low center of gravity make her a forgiving boat in the hands of a beginner. Her generous freeboard and side decks keep the crew on board and dry. Eight feet of cockpit and a large sun deck provide arm and leg room for four adults. Positive flotation is built in and a self-bailing cockpit gives still greater security. Don't let this tame exterior fool you, however, for the more experienced sailor, the **PRECISION 16** is a real performer.

She comes equipped with high quality rigging and includes kick-up rudder and centerboard. The **PRECISION 16** stacks up to be an excellent choice for you whether you are a first time sailor, weekend racer or a value conscious family.

Manufacturer: Precision Boat Works, 8517 Bradenton Road, Sarasota, FL 34243. 813/758-5611

SPECIFICATIONS: PRECISION 16
LOA: 16'3", LWL: 14', Beam: 6'8", Draft: board up - 8", board down - 3'8", Sail Area: Main - 97 s.f., Jib - 58 s.f., Weight: 390 lbs.

Approximate Price: $2800.

For the Sick

O God, who art always mindful of the sick and the discouraged, bless our comrades who are ill in the sick bay. Gladden their hearts with the sense of Thy mercy and deliver them from all worries and anxieties. Grant that they may endure suffering with holy patience, looking up to Thee. May calm fortitude take root and grow in the soil of their trouble. Amen.

PRECISION 16

INTERNATIONAL 505

"Calling the 505 a day sailer may be similar to calling the F-14 a nice little airplane." **This is what the class secretary, Dave Dussia, said when asked for information on the class for this book.**

Designed in 1954 by J. Westell, the **505** numbers over 8000 produced, with fleets around the world and still growing. She was originally call **Coronet**, a narrow 18-foot moulded plywood boat, with odd-looking flared gunwales. After proving to be a superior design in IYRU trials, the French Caneton Racing Association (one of the foremost small boat organizations in Europe) asked Mr. Westell to modify the **Coronet**. The new boat was six inches shorter at the bow and 12 inches shorter at the stern. It was first called the **Franco-British One Design**, but the new hull length (5.05 meters) inspired the present name.

The **505** is a high performance racing machine. It was not designed for easy sailing and requires strength, balance and skill to sail. If you can master this, you can sail one of the fastest racing dinghies in the world. If you're looking for excitement, contact this well organized class.
Class Association: International 505 Yacht Racing Association, Dave Dussia, Secretary, 5412 Greenfield Drive North, Portsmouth, VA 23703.

Manufacturer: International Sailing Products, Inc., P.O. Box 365, Oyster Bay, NY 11771. 516/922-5182

SPECIFICATIONS:
INTERNATIONAL 505
LOA: 16'6"
Weight: (minimum
 rigged) 280 lbs.
Sail Area:
 Main 100 s.f.
 Jib 75 s.f.
 Spinnaker 100 s.f.
Approximate Price: $7000+.

INTERNATIONAL 505

TOWN CLASS

The first **TOWN CLASS** was designed and built in 1932 by father and son, Marcus C. and Percival M. (Pert) Lowell. In 1936, the "townspeople's" boat debuted with its first class race in Marblehead, Massachusetts. Over 2000 of these classic daysailers have been produced. You can still purchase the **TOWN CLASS** in wood or fiberglass from the same place they have been made for over 50 years. The "Townie" is now being built by Pert and his son-in-law, Ralph Johnson.

This beautiful family daysailer will provide you, your children and grand children many years of great daysailing or racing. The **TOWN CLASS** has it all: lasting design, quality craftsmanship and quality materials.

If you are in the market for a safe, stable, classic daysailer, this might be the one.

Manufacturer: Pert Lowell, Co., Inc., Lane's End, Newbury Massachusetts 01950. 617/462-7409

SPECIFICATIONS:
TOWN CLASS
LOA: 16'6"
Beam: 5'9.5"
Freeboard: 21"
Draft:
 board up 7"
 board down 28"
Sail area: 152 s.f.
Weight:
 Wood 630 lbs.
 Fiberglass 800 lbs.
Mast: 24'
Boom: 12'

Approximate Price:
Wood - $6495.
Fiberglass - $8000.

TOWN CLASS

DAY SAILER 3

The **DAY SAILER 3** has been in production for over 28 years. Over 13,000 have been providing families and individual sailors enjoyment across the country.

The new **DAY SAILER 3** has the same basic hull shape and sail plan as the original fast, easily sailed, modest cost model. She carries a little higher freeboard aft, providing an even dryer cockpit. Many other improvements have been made in the cockpit and on deck to provide safer, more comfortable sailing.

The **DAY SAILER 3** is an easy to sail, easy to maintain, fast dinghy that was specifically designed for family daysailing. Three to five persons can sail in

DAY SAILER 3

comfort and still have plenty of room for camping or picnic gear.

Class Association: O'Day Owners' Association, 848 Airport Road, Fall River, Massachusetts 02720-4793.

Manufacturer: O'Day Sailboats, 848 Airport Road, Fall River, Massachusetts 02720-4793. 617/678-5291

SPECIFICATIONS:
DAY SAILER 3
LOA: 16'9"
LWL: 16'
Beam: 6'3"
Draft:
 board up 7"
 board down 3'9"
Sail Area: 145 s.f.
Mast Length: 24'3"
Hull Weight: 575 lbs.

Approximate
Price: $4100.

DAYSAILER I

Designed by Uffa Fox, the **DAYSAILER I** is the original daysailer. Previously manufactured by O'Day, this famous old original is now being produced by Precision Boat Works under license of the class association.

She is an outstanding family daysailer and racer. The roomy cockpit and large cuddy provide more than enough space for gear, camping equipment, lunch, the works!

For serious racing or just plain fun, **DAYSAILER I** is one of the best organized and well known classes in existence.

Class Association: Day Sailer Association, Dolores Bayer, P.O. Box 1918, Gulf Shores, Alabama 36542.

Manufacturer: Precision Boat Works, 8517 Bradenton Road, Sarasota, Florida 34243. 813/758-5611

SPECIFICATIONS:
DAYSAILER I
LOA: 16'9"
LWL: 16'
Beam: 6'3"
Draft:
  board up 7"
  board down 3'9"
Sail Area: 145 s.f.
Weight: 575 lbs.

Approximate
Price: $3995.

DAYSAILER I

DOLPHIN 17

At the present time, there are over 750 **DOLPHINS** in the fleet. Many are sailing in the Gulf of Mexico, as well as fresh water lakes throughout the country, and **DOLPHIN** is still known as the fastest and safest 17 foot daysailer.

The **DOLPHIN 17** is handcrafted fiberglass, has a reverse transom, two hundred pounds of ballast and top of the line hardware. Rigging has been reduced to light aluminum alloy, which has increased strength and decreased weight. This allows for more speed and maneuverability.

A partial listing of standard equipment found on the **DOLPHIN** 17 include kick-up rudder and centerboard, self bailing cockpit, storage, aft hatch, and even an ice box in the starboard hatch!!

The timeless hull design has proved to be one of the best. Custom or multi-color sails are available, as well as upholstery and exterior colors. Every boat is guaranteed 100% when it leaves the factory.

Manufacturer: Dolphin Enterprises, Inc., Route 2, Box 111A, Winslow, Arkansas 72959. 501/634-2541

SPECIFICATIONS:
DOLPHIN 17
LOA: 16'9"
Beam: 6'
Weight: 450 lbs.
Draft:
   board up 8"
   board down 4'3"
Sail Area: 160 s.f.

Approximate
Price: $4445

DOLPHIN 17

ISLANDS 17

The **ISLANDS 17** is designed for open water, bay or lake sailing. Her sloop rig produces performance under varied situations as a daysailer or racer.

She can be sailed easily, even single-handedly, but can handle six adults comfortably in her roomy cockpit. The **ISLANDS 17** is fast and planes with ease. She is stiff, stable and forgiving even for novice sailors. Her broad beam provides great stability and safety.

Her gunwales are flared for maximum spray deflection and rigidity. Large dry underdeck storage is available under the foredeck and in the lazerette aft. She has optional gear compartments under the port and starboard decks.

Constructed of Fiberglass, the **ISLANDS 17** features a complete liner with a self bailing cockpit. Her spars are made of black anodized aluminum and include spinnaker hardware, vang bails, downhall, outhaul and halyard cleats. For fast and easy placement, her mast step is hinged and can be taken down by one sailor.

Manufacturer: Sumner Boat Company, Inc., 334 S. Bayview Avenue, Amityville, NY 11701. 516/264-1830

SPECIFICATIONS:
ISLANDS 17
LOA: 16'9"
LWL: 15'10"
Beam: 6'6"
Draft:
  board up 7"
  board down 3'6"
Sail Area:
  Main 100 s.f.
  Jib 35 s.f.
Weight: 475 lbs.
Mast Height: 23'3"
Approximate
Price: $3595

KNOCKABOUT

The **17' Centerboard KNOCKABOUT** is from L. Francis Herreshoff's design number 39. She is an excellent example of the manner in which he combined grace of line with simplicity. She is an exciting daysailer, and because of her self-tending jib, she is an easy boat for one person to sail.

Bill Cannell and his fine craftsmen at the American Boat House build this lovely boat exactly to Herreshoff's plans, except for one detail. Rather than the split yoked tiller called for, they use a conventional tiller with hiking stick.

Quality building materials are used in this fine daysailer such as: white oak, locust, mahogany, cedar, pine, Sitka spruce, bronze, phosphor bronze and stainless steel.

Manufacturer: William B. Cannell Boatbuilding Co., Inc., American Boat House, Atlantic Avenue, P.O. Box 900, Camden, Maine 04843. 207/236-4188

SPECIFICATIONS: KNOCKABOUT
LOA: 16'10.5"
LWL: 13'11"
Draft: 4.25"
Weight: 450 lbs.
Sail Area: 124 s.f.

Approximate Price: Upon request

MOBJACK

For almost thirty years, the **MOBJACK** has provided Chesapeake's sailors fine daysailing and one-design racing. She was designed by Roger Moorman and later the designer's rights were obtained by the class association.

The **MOBJACK** is one of the best all-around boats her size. Her large "walk around" cockpit provides room for many when daysailing and allows for a sail handling from in the cockpit when racing and handling spinnaker. She is an exceptionally dry boat with plenty of flair topside, and high freeboard. She even offers a detachable

MOBJACK

cuddy for camping. She is self-bailing even with 1200 lbs. of crew aboard. She also offers furling jib and jiffy reefing main for safety and single-handed sailing.

The standard boat contains all the basic adjustments needed to learn to sail properly, including a traveler, outhaul, vang, and jib fairleads. Trapeze, spinnaker, etc. can be added when ready.

Manufacturer: Mobjack Systems, 11521 Danville Drive, Rockville, MD 20852. 301/881-7411

SPECIFICATIONS: MOBJACK
LOA: 17', LWL: 16'9", Beam: 6'6", Draft: board up 9", board down 4', Sail area: Main & Jib - 180 s.f., Spinnaker - 165 s.f.

Approximate Price: $4295.

SUPER RAY 17

Clearwater, Florida produced the **Optimist** and the **Windmill**, which have become standards. Has Glenn Henderson produced another Clearwater great? Yes!

Just one look at the **SUPER RAY 17** and you know this is no ordinary daysailer. From her elliptical center-

SUPER RAY 17

board, out to the tips of her dramatic "wings" and up to her tapered spar, you know she is designed to go. She draws attention wherever she goes.

The wings are needed to allow the crew weight to get out further from the center line and hold down the powerful sail plan. The wings are high enough to allow heeling up to 30 degrees without touching the water. If the **SUPER RAY** tries to roll out, the wings hit the water, keeping her stable.

If you've been into daysailing and are looking to moving up to something hotter (or maybe you want to start out in a hot one!) take a good look at the **SUPER RAY 17**.

Class Association: Super Ray Class Association, 14231 60th St. North, Clearwater, FL 33520.

Manufacturer: Super Ray Sailboats, 14231 60th Street North, Clearwater, FL 34620. 813/530-4277

Manufacturer's Rep.: Ron Meyer, 25836 Cordillera, Mission Viejo, CA 92691. 714/380-8818

SPECIFICATIONS:
SUPER RAY 17
LOA: 17'
LWL: 15'
Beam: 7'10"
Draft:
 board up 5"
 board down 4'
Hull Weight: 320 lbs.
Sail Area:
 Main 101 s.f.
 Jib 61 s.f.
 Spinnaker 192 s.f.

Approximate Price: $6900.

SWAMPSCOTT DORY

Pert Lowell's version of the **SWAMPSCOTT DORY** has more beam and one more plank per side. She is very similar to the old Coast Guard surf boats, and is available in sailing or rowing rigs.

She is a beautifully crafted boat. The stem, skeg, stern and frames are made of oak. Planking is all 5/8" and 7/8" pine. Trim and centerboard are oak and spars

are Alaskan Sitka spruce. All fittings are of the highest quality. This classic will provide many years of enjoyment.

Manufacturer: Pert Lowell, Co., Inc., Lane's End, Newbury, Massachusetts 01950. 617/462-7409

SWAMPSCOTT DORY

SPECIFICATIONS: SWAMPSCOTT DORY
LOA: 17', Beam: 4'8", Freeboard: 20", Draft: centerboard
up - 6", centerboard down - 20", Sail area: 74 s.f., Weight:
400 lbs.

Approximate Price: Sailing - $3600, Rowing - $2800.

THISTLE

"She must be big enough to carry a large party in reasonable comfort, small enough to fit into the average small garage, light enough for two men to be able to load her onto a trailer, and fast enough to give a good account of herself under all conditions. She must be reasonably dry and safer than the average. She must plane well and handle like a thoroughbred..."

With these thoughts, innovative dinghy sailor Sandy Douglass set about in 1945 to fashion a new boat -- a boat that, in her radical combination of features, would challenge many of the accepted marine design concepts of the day. She was to be a blend of high-performance racer and family daysailer, with abundant practical attributes as well.

Little surprise that Sandy's new boat, the **THISTLE**, was greeted initially with more skepticism than applause. (He is also the designer of the **Highlander**.) She did look different with her plumb bow and stern, round bilges and open foredeck. But it took just one race on a blustery day in Lake Erie to erase all hesitation, charting the **THISTLE** on a course that in succeeding years would lead her to acclaim by small-boat sailors nationwide as a standard of excellence in both design and construction.

Today, over forty years and 3800 **THISTLES** later, the same **THISTLE** design is still going strong...and fast. It is a source of class pride that in the decade of the 80's, **THISTLE** #1 continues to be an equal competitor with her newer, sleek fiberglass sister, and that #603 won the 1981 National Championships in her 25th year.

Class Association: Thistle Class Association, 1811 Cavell Avenue, Highland Park, Illinois 60035.

Manufacturer: Great Midwest Yacht Co., Box 364, 140 E. Granville St., Sunbury, Ohio 43074. 614/965-4511

THISTLE

SPECIFICATIONS: THISTLE
LOA: 17', LWL: 17', Beam 6', Draft: board up 9", board down 4'6", Hull Weight: 515 lbs., Sail Area: Main 136 s.f., Jib 55 s.f., Spinnaker 220 s.f., Capacity: Racing 3, Day-sailing up to 6.   **Approximate Price: $7250**

MUD HEN

The **MUD HEN** is a back-to-basics, sensible, no nonsense, small boat. With only 6" of draft (3'6" board down), she can sneak over the shallowest of sand bars into the coziest and most secluded of anchorages. She can be towed by most compacts and launched and recovered easily by a single person. The mast, mounted in its tabernacle (mast hinge), is quickly raised or lowered, and can be done while afloat, opening up cruising territories normally blocked by low fixed bridges. The experienced "*Henner*" can launch, step the mast, park the car and set sail (unaided) in less than 10 minutes.

The interior of the **MUD HEN** is functional and comfortable. Wide teak seats run fore and aft the full 11 foot length of the cockpit; a lift up seat forward has room to store a Porta-Potti underneath, and the optional dodger gives more than enough privacy, along with protection from the elements, and a place to sleep on the

MUD HEN

occasional overnight. Optional floorboards fill the footwell aft while sailing and lift up between the forward seats, making a queen-size sunbathing and sleeping area. Under the seats is room to store coolers, camping gear, provisions and fishing tackle. Aft, under the tiller, is the motor well which holds up to a 4 H.P. outboard, and allows it to tilt up out of the water for sailing and beaching. The high coamings provide ample back support, and the boom is high enough that the **MUD HEN** can be fitted with a Bimini top that has full sit up headroom; something really nice to have on a hot summer afternoon.

The best thing about a **MUD HEN** is her versatility. The number of uses to which she can be put is limited only by your imagination and sense of adventure.

The free standing cat rig is a study in simplicity. Reefing is quick and positive with built in jiffy reefing. Tacking is simply a matter of putting over the helm, changing sides only if wind conditions dictate. With the board fully lowered, the **MUD HEN** tacks an honest 90 degrees (45 degrees from the true wind). This is a great all around, recreational boat.

Manufacturer: Florida Bay Boat Company, 7095 S.W. 47th Street, Miami, FL 33155. 305/666-3003

SPECIFICATIONS: MUD HEN
LOA: 17'4", LWL: 16'3", Beam: 6'3", Draft: board up - 6", board down - 3'6", Weight: 650 lbs., Sail Area: 155 s.f., Capacity: 6 adults, Auxiliary: 2-4 H.P.

Approximate Price: $5950.

O Gracious Father, we are thankful for the labors of our messmen who prepare and serve our food. Watch over them and care for their loved ones. Amen.

FLEET-O-WING

This graceful keel knockabout was designed for Pert Lowell Co. in the 1930's by Sparkman and Stevens. The **FLEET-O-WING** is built to last and as sturdy as they come.

She enjoys a good run, and her enormous cockpit is great for a large day sailing party. There is ample space for six in this daysailer.

Construction is of classic high quality -- stem, stern keel and frames of mahogany, oak ribs and white pine planking. The deck is canvas covered marine plywood over oak carlines. The **FLEET-O-WING** has mast and

FLEET-O-WING

spars made of Sitka spruce, and she carries the finest hardware and rigging available.

Manufacturer: Pert Lowell Co., Inc., Lane's End, Newberry, Massachusetts 01950. 617/462-7409

SPECIFICATIONS: FLEET-O-WING
LOA: 17'9", LWL: 14'6", Beam: 6', Freeboard: 23", Draft: 3', Sail Area: 149 s.f., Hull Wt.: 1200 lbs.

Approximate Price: $16,000.

BUCCANEER

This thoroughbred racer was designed by Rod Macalpine Downie and Dick Gibbs, whose **Crossbow** holds the world's speed record for sailboats. The **BUCCANEER's** long, easy entry forward and broad flattened stern section makes her easily driven to windward and quick to plane, yet surprisingly stable and dry. Perfectly balanced, she sails with finger-tip touch. She carries a Portsmouth rating of 87.

A popular daysailer and racer, the **BUCCANEER** was originally built by Chrysler. The present builders have improved her and over 5000 are currently afloat with fleets from coast to coast. She carries modern rigging, including jib furling and a new fiberglass spinnaker launcher for easy, efficient sailing.

For just plain daysailing, the **BUCCANEER's** eight foot long cockpit, with comfortable seating and large storage area fore and aft, makes her a delight.

Class Association: Buccaneer Class Association, 735 Berkley Street, New Milford, NJ 07646.

Manufacturer: Contact Class Secretary, Linda Reitz, at 201/265-1819, for name of nearest manufacturer.

SPECIFICATIONS:
BUCCANEER
LOA: 18', LWL: 16'8",
Beam: 6', Draft: board
up 7", board down 3'10",
Weight: (rigged) 500 lbs.,
Sail Area: Main 114 s.f.,
Jib 61 s.f., Spinnaker
178 s.f.

Approximate Price:
Upon request.

BUCCANEER

ISLAND CREEK 18

The **ISLAND CREEK 18** captures the classic qualities of the Jersey beach skiff with modern materials and traditional craftsmanship. Features that make her ideal for trailering or beaching include her unstayed mast, long keel and retractable centerboard. The mast and sails stow neatly inside the deck. Her straight keel is wide enough to enable her to sit upright on a beach.

Her hull, floating chambers and centerboard assembly are all made of hand laminated Fiberglass. There is no encapsulated wood anywhere in these laminates. This feature eliminates the potential of rot damage within the hull unit.

The deck is strip planked cedar, trimmed with white oak, or locust rub rail, toe rail and coaming. The sprit and hollow mast are built of Sitka spruce for strength and lightness. Endseats, thwarts and centerboard cap are Douglas fir. The redwood floor boards are unvarnished for a non-skid surface.

Sails and running rigging on the **ISLAND CREEK** are Dacron.

The quality craftsmanship of this boat is unsurpassed. The people at **Island Creek Boat Services** are designers and builders, as well as sailors and know what is needed and expected in fine sailing craft.

Manufacturer: Island Creek Boat Services, George Surgent, Designer & Builder, Box 151, Williams Wharf Road, St. Leonard, Maryland 20685. 301/586-1893

SPECIFICATIONS: ISLAND CREEK 18
LOA: 18', LWL: 16', Beam: 5'4", Draft: board up - 1', board down - 2'6", Sail Area: 118 s.f., Displacement: 1300 lbs.

Approximate Price: $6750.

ISLAND CREEK 18

MERCURY CLASS YACHT

"A practical boat for all weather sailing..at a moderate price" is just as true today as it was in the early 1940's when Ernest Nunes was advertising his new **MERCURY** design in Sausalito, California.

Designed for the rugged conditions of San Francisco Bay in summer, the **MERCURY** proved to be equally at home in the very light air of Carmel. As a result of this

versatility, the **MERCURY** is found up and down the Pacific Coast from San Diego to Seattle, including several lakes and rivers.

The original **MERCURY** could be purchased as a plywood kit for home assembly, partially assembled waiting to be finished, or complete and ready to sail. To this day, plans are available from the Association for the home builder.

MERCURY CLASS YACHT

After twenty years of plywood only construction, the MCYRA made the bold decision to authorize the building of fiberglass **MERCURYS** by a franchised boat builder. The idea, while controversial at the time, proved a boost to the class. Not only was the **MERCURY** now low maintenance with major repairs completed with amazing ease, the boats became relatively inexpensive and were uniformly well built.

Another major step was taken in 1970 when the Association allowed the use of tubular aluminum spars. It was at this time point that the class evolved into the sophisticated realm of sailboat racing. Now, not only was the mast more controllable, it was stronger. The sailmaking technology of other "development" classes was utilized making the **MERCURY** even more popular with serious racing sailors. The advent of mechanical pushers in 1979 added to the new sophistication.

Contrary to the trend in other classes, The Mercury Association has insisted that the boats be well built, durable and safe. As a result, with the advent of sealed bulkheads, the seaworthy **MERCURY** has become even safer. It is also not unusual to see wooden boats and the original fiberglass boats among the highest finishers in any regatta.

Class Association: Mercury Class Yacht Racing Association, Phyllis Baird, 694 W. Morris Street, Fresno, CA 93704.

Manufacturer: Moore Boats, 1650 Commercial, Santa Cruz, CA 95065. 415/324-1311 or 415/368-4027 (evenings)

SPECIFICATIONS: MERCURY CLASS YACHT
LOA: 18', LWL: 13', Beam: 5'4", Draft: 3'1", Weight: 1100 lbs. (min.).

Approximate Price: $8500.

RHODES 18

It's fast, exciting, and above all, a safe boat for racing or family daysailing. There are few boats available with such a comfortably large and deep cockpit as this Philip Rhodes designed 18-footer.

The large foredeck provides ample room to handle jibs, mooring or anchor lines, and a more than adequate space below for life jackets, anchor and line, lunch baskets, camping gear, and even space for a small bunk.

The **RHODES 18** is an ideal family daysailer, splendid for gunkholing, racing, or camping and can be easily sailed by two. For the racing enthusiast, the **RHODES 18** comes equipped with two-part jib sheets for ease of handling, adjustable backstay and internal halyards. Spinnakers and Genoas are available as extra equipment.

As standard equipment, the **RHODES 18** comes equipped with Zephyr tapered anodized aluminum mast, roller reefing, stainless steel standing rigging, swedged stainless turnbuckles, boom crutch, non-skid deck surface, and is available in either the keel or centerboard models. The keel is cast iron and bolted through the hull with six half-inch stainless bolts. This enables the keel to be easily removed for storage or shipping. The centerboard model has a half-inch steel centerboard with a differential centerboard winch which can be operated with safety and ease by a youngster.

The fittings on the **RHODES 18** are stainless steel and varnished. Running rigging is Dacron.

Manufacturer: Cape Cod Shipbuilding Co., Narrows Road, Box 152, Wareham, MA 02571. 617/295-3550

SPECIFICATIONS: RHODES 18
LOA: 18', LWL: 16', Beam: 6'3", Draft: board up - 7", board down - 4', Draft: Keel Model 32", Sail Area: 162 s.f., Weight: Keel Model - 920 lbs., C/B Model - 800 lbs., Keel Weight Cast Iron: 300 lbs. **Approximate Price:** $7634.

RHODES 18

SAILING SURF DORY 18

This beautiful dory is being produced by Jim Odell and his son George at the same shop that was producing

them about 200 years ago in Amesbury, Massachusetts. This is the oldest continuously operated boat shop in the

SAILING SURF DORY 18

United States. The Lowell Boat Shop was founded in 1793.

Pine planking, oak frames and gunwales, and mahogany through most of the remaining structure make for a beautiful and long-lasting classic. The **SAILING SURF DORY 18** offers almost any sail rig, but the usual rigs are the gunter or sprit. For auxiliary power, there are three sets of oarlocks which permit double rowing or single rowing from different positions or an outboard motor box is fitted inside the transom out of the way.

Lowell's Boat Shop also offers the dory in 14' to 20' lengths. The 18 footer will seat 4 to 6 persons and not be crowded. If you're interested in one of the classics for daysailing, be sure to look at these.

Manufacturer: Lowell's Boat Shop, 459 Main Street, Amesbury, MA 01913. 617/388-0162

SPECIFICATIONS: SAILING SURF DORY 18
LOA: 18', Beam: 6', Weight: 500 lbs., Sail Area: 120 s.f., Draft: board up 5", board down 44"

Approximate Price: $9000

During Foreign Travel

We thank Thee, O God, for the privilege of visiting far away lands. How strange are the canoes of the primitives, the junks of the Pacific, the peculiar habits and the different forms of speech. As we visit other nations, give us a respect for their ways and customs. Let no careless word cause ill will and give wrong impressions. O God, help us to be ambassadors of good will in all our travels. Amen.

Y-FLYER

This is a fast, simple, stable boat designed for high performance and family fun. It even has an excellent class-supported do-it-yourself program for the sailor who prefers to build his own. The **Y-FLYER** is a great boat for beginners and experienced racers. America's Cup winner, Ted Turner, is a past national champion.

This is a well-organized, fun class with approximately 20 active fleets in the U.S. Family crews make up a large part of the fleets. Many of their national championships are won by family or all-woman teams. The strict one-design class keeps the older boats equal. There

Y-FLYER

is no trapeze and no spinnaker in the U.S., so you don't have to worry about being a super athlete to sail her.

At 18', the **Y-FLYER** is no tiny dinghy. Even though two can race it, five or six can get in the large cockpit for pleasure sailing with a cooler and sandwiches.

The cost is very reasonable. The class reports that you can build a new boat for as little as $4000. There are two fiberglass builders available, as well.

Go for it! The **Y-FLYER** leaves you no excuses. Contact the class secretary.

Class Association: American Y-Flyer Yacht Racing Association, 489 Redwood Forest Drive, Manchester, Missouri 63021.

Manufacturer: Turner Marine, P.O. Box 641, Neoga, IL 62447. 217/895-2277

Manufacturer: L.E. Lundquist & Co., Rte. 2, Box 60DD, Ninety-Six, SC 29666. 803/227-1874

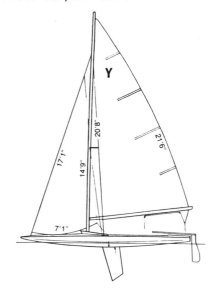

SPECIFICATIONS:
Y-FLYER
LOA: 18'
LWL: Flat - 14'6"
   Heeled - 16'8"
Beam: 5'8"
Draft:
  board up 6"
  board down 4'
Sail Area:
  Main 110 s.f.
  Jib 51 s.f.
Min. Weight fully
  rigged: 500 lbs.

Approximate
Price: $6000.

NAIAD

Early in 1985, the late Gordon Fisher approached designer Mark Ellis to discuss an idea. Mr. Fisher wanted a small traditional catboat for his personal use on Lake Memphremagog in the Eastern Townships of Quebec. The requirements were very specific; the boat must be easily ramp launched, she would be ballasted for stability under sail and on her mooring, she must be very comfortable to sit in and easy to sail alone, she would, of course, be self-bailing and unsinkable, she must be "spare", (a characteristic requirement of Mr. Fisher) in that she would be devoid of un-useful features, and, perhaps above all, she must be of traditional appearance and uncommon beauty.

The collaboration between visionary Gordon Fisher and designer Mark Ellis had, in a similar fashion, led to the remarkable **Nonesuch** design some years earlier.

Mr. Fisher's little catboat was called **NAIAD**, and she became a reality in the summer of 1985. Beautifully crafted in cold-moulded cedar, the first **NAIAD** graced

NAIAD

the lagoons of the Toronto Islands through the late summer and fall, and all who saw her could testify that the requirements set down had been realized, perhaps beyond expectations.

Luna Yachts now presents **NAIAD** in hand-laid fiberglass construction, faithful to the original classic lines with shapely wineglass transom, and beautifully varnished laminated wood trim in mahogany and ash. She is built with care and pride, by one of the finest small boat shops in North America.

Manufacturer: Luna Yachts, Ltd., Unit 20, 427 Speers Road, Oakville, Ontario, Canada L6K 3S8. 416/842-4808

SPECIFICATIONS:
NAIAD
LOA: 18'3"
LWL: 17'6"
Beam: 6'
Draft:
  board up 8"
  board down 3'8"
Displacement:
  1300 lbs.
Ballast: 500 lbs.
Sail Area: 144 s.f.

Approximate
Price: $8200

BEACHCOMBER DORY 18

A modern adaptation of the famed **New England Dory**, the **BEACHCOMBER DORY** blends the qualities of tradition and the advantages of modern technology with her fiberglass hull and inboard or outboard power.

She is designed to be sailed right onto the beach or worked in shallow water. The dory has always been famous for handling rough water in coastal waterways. The motor is mounted in a well and tilts up for beaching or docking.

The **BEACHCOMBER**'s sprit sail rig carries main and jib. The unstayed rig can be set up quickly and the entire rig can be stowed in the boat for trailering. A contemporary sloop rig is also offered.

BEACHCOMBER DORY 18

For camping or gunkholing weekends, she offers a forward section option with cover and cushioned 7' berths. The cover fits around the mast and she can be sailed with the cover up. The **BEACHCOMBER DORY** is a good all-around sailing, fishing and camping boat for shallow inland waters.

Manufacturer: Beachcomber Fiberglass Technology, 2850 S.E. Market Place, Stuart, Florida 34997. 305/283-0200, 546-5692

SPECIFICATIONS: BEACHCOMBER DORY
LOA: 18'4", LWL" 15'2", Beam: 6', Sail Area: 135 s.f., Draft: centerboard up 6", centerboard down 3'6", Weight: 550 lbs.

Approximate Price: $6350.

BUZZARDS BAY 19

This is an enlarged version of the well-known 17' **Concordia Sloop** designed by R.D. "Pete" Culler. The **BUZZARDS BAY 19** is one of his last designs and came at the request of a customer who felt he needed a larger and more stable daysailer for the Buzzards Bay-Vineyard Sound area, which is rough sailing at times.

The **BUZZARDS BAY 19** is an all wood classic beauty. The Landing School of Boat Building and Design uses this boat as a means of teaching students the disciplines of the wooden boatbuilding trade. The boats they produce are a masterpiece of all wood construction.

For the daysailer enthusiast who prefers classic wood beauty, the **BUZZARDS BAY 19** may be the best of all worlds. She is stable, roomy, fast and responsive in light or heavy air. She will draw attention wherever she sails.

Manufacturer: The Landing School of Boat Building and Design, P.O. Box 1490, Kennebunkport, Maine 04046. 207/985-7976

SPECIFICATIONS:
BUZZARDS BAY 19
LOA: 18'8"
Beam: 6'8"
Draft:
 board up 2'
 board down 4'
Sail Area: 192 s.f.
Weight: 2300 lbs.

Approximate
Price: $9500.

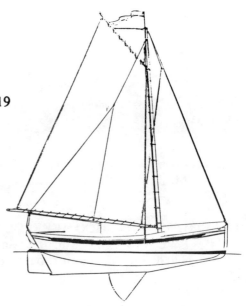

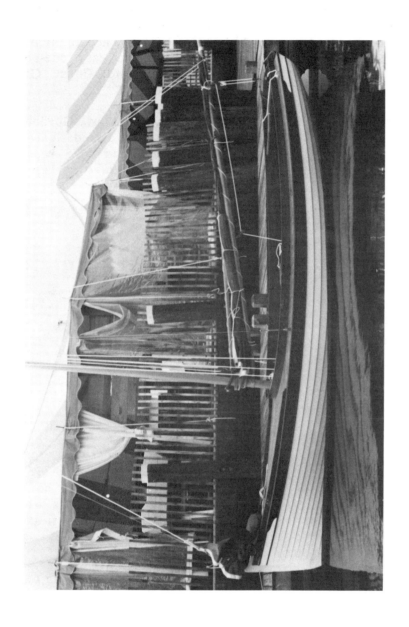

FLYING SCOT

There is no other daysailer that offers the combination of stability, simplicity, exceptional roominess, abundant storage space and a great planing hull for performance like the **FLYING SCOT**. The simplicity of rigging and trailering makes sailing an easy one-person situation, yet is family oriented and Coast Guard approved for eight persons.

The **FLYING SCOT** was designed by Gordon K. "Sandy" Douglass over 30 years ago (who also designed the **Thistle** and **Highlander**). With more than 4375 boats on the water, the **FLYING SCOT** is one of the best all-around daysailers ever produced.

She is not just a family racing class. She boasts a Mallory Cup winner, two Adams Cup winners and a USYRU champion. The class is one of the largest in the country, with over 130 racing fleets. She is easily trailered to distant regattas.

The **FLYING SCOT** is a safe boat. You can walk around on deck and she remains stable. She will not

FLYING SCOT is a Registered Trademark.

FLYING SCOT

sink; even when filled with water, a man can stand and walk on deck when swamped.

If you're looking for a family daysailer/racer, or if you've learned in one of the small, cramped daysailers and are looking for something bigger, this could be the right boat for you. The **FLYING SCOT** is worth investigating.

Class Association: Flying Scot Sailing Association, J. Edgar Eubanks, Secretary, 3008 Millwood Avenue, Columbia, SC 29205.

Manufacturer: Gordon Douglass Boat Co., Inc., Rt. 4, Box 9K, Cemetery St., Deer Park, MD 21550. 301/334-4848

Manufacturer: The WestScot Corp., 1006 W. Beardsley Place, Salt Lake City, UT 84119. 801/972-0350

SPECIFICATIONS: FLYING SCOT
LOA: 19', LWL: 18'6", Beam: waterline 6'9", deck edge 7'1.25", Draft: board up 8", board down 4', Hull Wt.: 675 lbs., Sail Area: Main & Jib 190 s.f., Spinnaker 200 s.f.

Approximate Price: $7500 (Trailer included)

FLYING SCOT is a Registered Trademark.

LIGHTNING

The best of both worlds. This class has provided great racing and comfortable daysailing for 50 years. Designed by Olin Stephens, the nineteen foot **LIGHTNING** was developed to bridge the gap that existed between the small 14 to 16 foot one-designs and the larger, expensive standard meter classes. With about 14,000 boats now registered, and a very strong class association, this is one of the most successful designs.

The original wooden design was to accommodate ease of construction for home builders using low-cost materials. Most **LIGHTNINGS** are of fiberglass today, but her simple angular lines are still there. All boats produced today are designed for full flotation and can be self-rescuing. The practical rig carries 177 s.f. of sail plus a 300 s.f. spinnaker. She is fast, but retains very good helm balance in most sailing positions.

A racing crew of three is needed, but the large cockpit will hold 5-6 for daysailing. This is a great all-around boat, and the class is well organized and offers fleets worldwide.

Class Association: International Lightning Class Association, 808 High Street, Worthington, Ohio 43085.

Manufacturer: Allen Boat Co., 655 Fuhrman Blvd., Buffalo, NY 14203. 716/842-0800
Manufacturer: Fuzzy Specialties, Jim Carson, 499 Princeton Avenue, Brick, NJ 08724. 201/892-1924
Manufacturer: McLaughlin Boat Works, 4737 Adams Rd., Hixson, TN 37343. 615/875-4040
Manufacturer: Mueller Boat Co., 1809 Root Rd., Lorain, Ohio 44052. 216/288-0002
Manufacturer: Nickels Boat Works, 2426 S. Long Lake Rd., Fenton, MI 48430. 313/750-1855

SPECIFICATIONS: LIGHTNING
LOA: 19', LWL: 15'3", Beam: 6'6", Draft: board up - 5", board down - 4'11", Displacement: 700 lbs., Sail Area: 177 s.f.   **Approximate Price: $8000.**

LIGHTNING

RHODES 19

The **RHODES 19** was first produced in the mid-1940's as a post-war product for the Allied Aviation Corp., which had produced molded plywood aircraft fuselages. This Phillip Rhodes designed sloop was then called the **Hurricane.**

After the failure of Allied, a New Bedford builder, Palmer Scott, began producing the boat under the name **SMYRA.** Southern Massachusetts Yacht Racing Association chose the design because of its ability to handle the broad range of sailing conditions in the Cape Cod area. The SMYRA was produced in fiberglass (after two or three manufacturing changes) by O'Day, who in 1958 agreed with Phil Rhodes to use his name to identify the boat. She is now being produced by Stuart Marine in Maine.

Over the years, more than 3,000 of these fine, daysailer/racers have been produced. In the late 1960's, she won *Yachting Magazine*'s heavy air, one-of-a-kind

RHODES 19

regatta. The Class Association is well-organized and has active fleets in New England, Chicago, Louisiana and Long Island.

The **RHODES 19** being presently produced is of very high quality and beautifully finished. She is available in both fixed keel or centerboard and can be rigged with all the goodies for racing. She has a very large, comfortable cockpit for daysailing a group. There is more than enough storage room in the lockable cuddy. This boat is impressive. Check it out if you're looking for one of the larger daysailers.

Class Association: Rhodes 19 Class Association, George G. Lail, Secretary, 22 West Shore Drive, Marblehead, MA 01945.

Manufacturer: Stuart Marine Corp., 633 Route One, Rockport, ME 04856. 207/236-8053

SPECIFICATIONS:
RHODES 19
LOA: 19'2"
LWL: 17'9"
Beam: 7'
Sail Area: Main
 and Jib 175 s.f.
Draft:
 Keel Model 3'3"
 C/B Model:
  board up 10"
  down 4'11"
Weight:
 C/B Model
  1050 lbs.
 Keel Model
  1325 lbs.

Approximate Price: $7000.

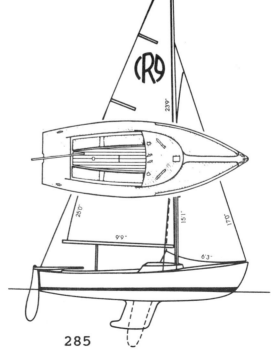

285

INTERNATIONAL FLYING DUTCHMAN

The **FLYING DUTCHMAN (FD)** was designed by U. van Essen in 1951. Since 1960, she has been an Olympic class. For over 35 years, she has been acclaimed the ultimate in dinghy racing by her admirers.

This sloop-rigged daysailer is stable and relatively easy to sail, but must be skillfully managed with perfect teamwork by her two-man crew to get the most out of her. She has a powerful rig and planing hull. Strength, agility and cunning are needed to bring home the trophy in any **FD** regatta.

Over 10,000 **FD's** have been built and more than 2500 are actively racing in 40 countries. You can even build it yourself, with the help of plans from the class association. This class is international and well-organized.

If you're in good physical shape and are looking for the ultimate in high performance dinghy racing, look over the **FLYING DUTCHMAN**.

Class Association: IFDCAUS, Peter Wells, Secretary/Treasurer, P.O. Box 152, Rindge, NH 03461.

Manufacturer: KDV-USA, Inc., 117 Pear Tree Point Road, Darien, CT 06820

Manufacturer: Mark Lindsay Boatbuilders, 30 Blackburn Center, Gloucester, MA 01930.

SPECIFICATIONS:
FLYING DUTCHMAN
LOA: 19'10"
Beam: 5'11"
Draft: 3'8"
Sail Area: 190 s.f.

Approximate Price:
$10,000 to $12,000.

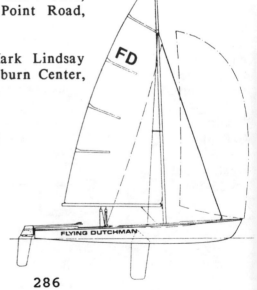

INTERNATIONAL FLYING DUTCHMAN

DINGHIES AND DAYSAILERS /
20' To 38'

C SCOW

Because of her versatility, this highly maneuverable cat-rigged scow has been the most popular of all scows over the years. As an exciting tactical racer for 2-3 people, the **C SCOW** has plenty of sophisticated gear and enjoys dozens of very competitive racing fleets around the country with many regattas held throughout the season. Yet, she is easily skippered by one and is roomy enough to take a few non-sailor friends out for a fun afternoon of daysailing.

The **C SCOW** has been around since 1908 and is one of the classes represented by the Inland Lake Yachting Association, which is approximately 4000 strong. This is one of the best organized class associations, which provides good competition and comraderie.

Beautiful, fun, exciting -- the **C SCOW** has been providing sailors with pleasure for almost 80 years.

C SCOW

Class Association: Inland Lake Yachting Association, P.O. Box 311, Fontana, Wisconsin 53125. 414/275-6921

Manufacturer: Melges Boat Works, Inc., Zenda, Wisconsin 53195. 414/248-6621

Manufacturer: Johnson Boat Works, 4495 Lake Ave., White Bear Lake, MN 55110. 612/429-7221

SPECIFICATIONS
C SCOW
LOA: 20'
Beam: 7'
Sail Area:
  216 s.f.
Hull Weight:
  650 lbs.

Approx. Price
$8850-$8999

Upon Launching a Ship

O Almighty God, the Sovereign Commander of all the World, whose command even the wind and sea obey, we look to Thee, as we gather to launch this vessel of the United States Navy. We ask Thy blessing upon this occasion. Grant that this ship will always travel in peaceful waters, but if armed conflict is thrust upon us, may she bring credit to the great traditions of our Navy. Bless the officers and men who will sail her on the high seas. May they see the wonders of the deep and always invite Thy hand to steady the wheel. Conduct in safety the voyages of this ship and may we express our thankfulness for Thy merciful providence by a constant devotion to duty and a sincere faith in Thee. Amen.

HIGHLANDER

Big, fast and good looking, the **HIGHLANDER** is a beauty for racing and daysailing. She is 20 feet in length and has a large 11-foot by five foot cockpit. Ten can go for a fun sail in the **HIGHLANDER**, but she can be handled easily by two for racing or daysailing. Her size also makes her great for camping trips.

At 830 lbs. and 225 s.f. of sail area, combined wit a long water line and a planing hull, she is designe to go **fast**. HIGHLANDER, designed by Gordon Douglass

HIGHLANDER

consistently places in one of the top positions in *Yachting Magazine's* "One-Of-A-Kind Regatta".

The **HIGHLANDER** Class Association is a little unusual, in that they purchased the rights to the boat from it's original owners. This assures stability of the design and quality of construction.

She trailers easily, making the rental of a slip unnecessary. So, follow the racing circuit or take the family out for a fun sail in the lakes.

Class Association: Highlander Class International Association, 4920 Mary Brook Drive, Kettering, Ohio 45429.
Manufacturer: Customflex, Inc., 1817 Palmwood Av., Toledo, Ohio 43607. 419/536-4693

SPECIFICATIONS:
HIGHLANDER
LOA: 20'
LWL: 19'8"
Beam: 6'8"
Draft:
 board up 8"
 board down 5'6"
Sail Area:
 Main & Jib
  225 s.f.
 Spinnaker
  250 s.f.
Displacement:
 830 lbs.

Approximate
Price: $7000

M-20 SCOW

The high-performance **M-20** with its slightly tunneled hull and modern, high aspect ratio rig is one of the sportiest of the scows. While it is raced with only two average sized adults (or 2-3 smaller ones), the great number of adjustments available, including spinnaker gear, keep the crew as well as the skipper busier than on any other scow. Fast and responsive, it requires both to be "on their toes".

The **M-20** is represented by two associations and ha been growing since its beginning 25 years ago. These ar well organized and offer great competition and comra derie.

Whether in a light breeze or a heavy blowing wind this scow will satisfy *and challenge* the best of sailors.

M-20 SCOW

Class Association: M20 Sailing Association, 1720 Jackson St., La Crosse, WI 54601.

Class Association: Inland Lake Yachting Association, P.O. Box 311, Fontana, WI 53125 414/275-6921

Manufacturer: Melges Boat Works, Zenda, WI 53195. 414/248-6621

Manufacturer: Johnson Boat Works, 4495 Lake Avenue, White Bear Lake, MN 55110. 612/429-7221

SPECIFICATIONS:
M20 SCOW
LOA: 20'
LWL: 14'
Beam: 5'8"
Draft: 3'6"
Sail Area:
 Main & Jib:
  176 s.f.
 Spinnaker:
  200 s.f.
Hull Wt.: 595 lbs.

Approx. Price:
9000-$9135

Forgive us, Our Heavenly Father, of the sins which follow us through the day into the night. Enable us to bridle our passions that we may control ourselves. We are ashamed in Thy presence as we remember our idle gossip, our unfair advantage, our narrow condemnation of our shipmates. Keep us from thoughts of revenge lest we taint ourselves with the poison of hatred. Enable us to love even at the cost of our pride, for Thou didst first love us. Amen.

YNGLING

Designed by Jan H. Linge in the late 1960's, the **YNGLING** resembles her famous big sister, the **Soling**. But she is more docile, has more beam, higher freeboard with more sheer and fuller body lines. She was designed as a training boat for her larger sister and for juniors. (YNGLING means "youngster" in Norwegian). She has since gained a name of her own and has an organized International Class and fleets around the world. This individual success is probably attributed to her being a sophisticated sailer that does not require a group of professional "rock stars" to crew her.

The **YNGLING** has a ballast/displacement ratio of 51%, which gives her outstanding stability. She is said to have unmatched pointing ability. This self-righting boat is designed with ample flotation to insure safety and is reportedly capable of handling a 30 to 40 knot gale.

All of these attributes add up to a fine daysailer that can be sailed by one or two, or more, whether your interest be racing or just family pleasure sailing.

Class Association: North American Yngling Association, 1461 Bay Ridge Road, Wayzata, MN 55391.

Manufacturer: Scandia Plast Boat Works, P.O. Box 515, Station E, Victoria, B.C., Canada V8W-2NB. 604/652-0544

SPECIFICATIONS:
YNGLING
LOA: 20'9"
LWL: 15'5"
Beam: 5'8"
Draft: 3'6"
Freeboard: 1'7"
Weight: 1320 lbs.
Iron keel: 680 lbs.
Sail Area: 150 s.f.

Approximate Price: $10,940

YNGLING

IMPULSE 21

"More Fun and Less Fuss." That's what this beautiful Bill Cook design has achieved. No hiking straps or trapeze, and yet a go fast daysailer that can be sailed by the average sailor. The 600 pound keel handles stability and the powerful fractional rig, carrying 208 s.f. of sail area, provides performance.

I like the self tacking jib and center mounted console, where most control lines are led, allowing for a very organized cockpit. All the standing and running rigging is top-notch on the **IMPULSE 21**. The spinnaker is launched through a tube *Fire-ball* style.

The cockpit is very large and comfortable, and the cuddy cabin provides ample storage for summer outings. The raked transom with platform built-in is great for snorkeling or swimming.

The **IMPULSE 21** is a great boat for all-around day sailing and racing for any sailor that can't or doesn't want to be a gorilla or acrobat in order to go fast and have fun.

Manufacturer: Impulse Marine, 12880 Hillcrest Road, Suite 236, Dallas, Texas 75230. 214/980-2438

SPECIFICATIONS:
IMPULSE 21
LOA: 21'
LWL: 18'
Draft: 3'5"
Displacement:
 1300 lbs.
Ballast: 600 lbs.
Sail Area: 208 s.f.

Approximate
Price: $11,500

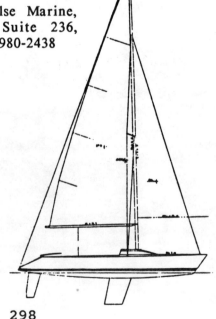

IMPULSE 21

SEA PEARL 21

At first glance, it may appear a little strange, but this cat/ketch rigged beauty is fast and seaworthy, as well as simple and easy to rig.

N. L. Herreshoff designed the original **SEA PEARL** around 1930. Marine Concepts has produced the **SEA PEARL 21**, based on that original and offers it in both Marconi and twin lug rigs.

She features a large self-bailing cockpit aft of the mizzen and a large storage compartment forward. The forward storage compartment can be used as a footwell for daysailing or as a shelter for eating/sleeping, with the optional canvas cabin cover. All this storage and camping area, along with a six inch draft, makes it a great gunkholing boat.

She's a well constructed boat and finished beautifully. Easy to trailer, rig and sail.

Manufacturer: Marine Concepts, 159 Oakwood Street East, Tarpon Springs, FL 34689. 813/937-0166

SPECIFICATIONS:
SEA PEARL 21
LOA: 21'
LWL: 19'
Beam: 5'6"
Draft:
 board up 6"
 board down 2'6"
Displacement:
 550 lbs.
Sail Area: 136 s.f.

**Approximate
Price:** $5400.

SEA PEARL 21

X21

In the late 1960's, Beckmann Christensen saw a need for a compact, economical keelboat for daysailing and racing by a family. He wanted it faster than a **Rhodes 19** or **Ensign**, but comfortable and easy to sail. He took this concept to designer Tom Norton and they Produced the first **X21** in 1972.

They produced a gem. The **X21** is a classic example of form following function. She has the look of a proper yacht. She resembles a junior offshore racer and sails with the grace of a 12-meter. Her performance is dazzling enough for the most blase hot-shot, yet she is friendly to the novice sailor. (She's been used as a trainer by North American Sailing Center). Sailing the X21 provides a positive sense of security and comfort, while at the same time providing an exhilarating sense of speed and power.

Manufacturer: Perkins Boat Co., P.O. Box C-447, Westport, MA 02790. 617/636-2250

SPECIFICATIONS:
X21
LOA: 21'
LWL: 17'6"
Beam: 6'6"
Draft: 4'
Displacement:
 2400 lbs.
Ballast: 1200 lbs.
Sail Area: 191 s.f.

Approximate
Price: $15,000.

X21

WHITEHALL 22

Patterned after the original **WHITEHALL 12** which dates back to Colonial times, this sailing/rowing boat is

a classic. Because it is constructed of fiberglass instead of wood, they were able to change the lines a little.

WHITEHALL 22

With the **WHITEHALL** 22-footer you have a boat that can be rowed by an eight-man crew, sailed with a gaff rig, or powered by outboard. The floorboards on this boat can be lifted to create a deck for sleeping. A tent which uses the oars as a ridge pole is available. This boat is designed to be easily trailered, launched and rigged.

Varnished mahogany gunwales, spruce seats and floor boards and stainless shrouds are some of the fine quality materials used in the **WHITEHALL 22**.

Manufacturer: B&S Corp., Harrison C. Sylvester, Bessey Ridge Road, Albion, Maine 04910. 207/437-9245

SPECIFICATIONS: WHITEHALL 22
LOA: 22', Beam 6'6", Weight: 1200 lbs., Draft: 4', Sail Area: 215 s.f.

Approximate Price: $11,000

For Independence Day

Almighty and everlasting God, Thou who has given us this great Nation, make us aware of all the solemn responsibilities which we face in defending our great heritage of freedom. Keep us from shirking our duties for "we are now testing whether this nation or any other nation so conceived and dedicated, can long endure". Without a real dependence in Thee we will surely fail. Bless all our people with good manners, brotherly love, and a peaceful unity that we may strengthen the foundations of the people's republic. Enable our President, and those in political authority to do their work with wisdom and justice. In the time of trial, be Thou our Protector and Defender. Amen.

ENSIGN

The **ENSIGN** is the largest class of full keel, one-design sailboats in the United States, with 44 active fleets and many non-fleet members. She was designed by Carl Alberg as the **Electra Day Sailer**, and was first produced in 1962. Shortly thereafter, the class association and name changed to **ENSIGN**, and she gained popularity fast. Over 1000 were produced by the end of 1965.

ENSIGN is a beautiful daysailer/racer. She is stable and has a very large cockpit and cuddy.

The **ENSIGN** Class Association is well organized and offers great racing and comraderie.

Class Association: Ensign Class Association, Noreen Collins, 7341 Briarwood Drive, Mentor, Ohio 44060.

SPECIFICATIONS:
ENSIGN
LOA: 22'6"
LWL: 16'9"
Beam: 7'
Draft: 3'
Weight: 3000 lbs.
Ballast: 1200 lbs.
 lead
Sail Area:
 Main 140 s.f.
 Jib 61 s.f.
 Genoa #1 150 s.f.
 Genoa #2 111 s.f.

Approximate Price:
Upon request.

ENSIGN

STAR

The **STAR** was designed by Francis Sweisguth in 1910. Five raced in the 1911 Memorial Day Regatta of the Harlem Yacht Club. For over 75 years, the **STAR** Class has remained strong. Over 7000 **STARS** have been registered over the years, and there are organized fleets in 20 countries today. This is without a doubt the most famous class of one-design.

Many rigging and construction changes have been made since the first **STAR**, but the changes have been slow and only reflect changes that benefit the class. The **STAR** Class Association is the example for one-design associations.

No matter how good the association, the **STAR** would not have lasted unless it was a great boat - IT IS! It is a complicated racing machine and not normally the choice of a novice sailor.

If you're already a sailor and looking to move into one of the more sophisticated sailing machines, do look the **STAR** over.

Class Association: International Star Class Yacht Racing Association, 1545 Waukegan Rd., Ste. 8, Glenview, Illinois 60025-2185.
Manufacturer: Exact Boat Co., Inc., 2827 Buren St., Camden, NJ 08105. 609/541-6800
Manufacturer: William Buchan, 4025 94th N.E., Bellevue, WA 98004.
Manufacturer: Rolland Vortriede, 1730 Burns, Detroit, MI 48214.
Manufacturer: William J. Matson Co., 516 Palm Av., Carpinteria, CA 93013.

SPECIFICATIONS: STAR
LOA: 22' 8 1/2", Beam: 5' 8 1/4", Draft: 3'4", Weight: 1479 lbs., Mast from deck to measurement band: 31'8", Sail Area: 87 s.f.

Approximate Price: $21,500 (includes trailer).

SONAR

SONAR was specifically designed to the desired features by Bruce Kirby (also designer of the **Laser**). She can be sailed by young or old, by couples, or by the entire family.

The **SONAR** has a very specific purpose -- to get more sailors off the beach and on the water.

She is an exceptionally fast, high performance one-design that has given some flat-out racers in the Olympics classes a run for their money.

This boat features the finest of standard equipment and rigging, which also includes spinnaker gear. There's plenty of stowage with three cockpit lockers and locking cabin.

SONAR is also a comfortable, stable and simple daysailer that gets families and friends out on the water together for a pleasant day's sail.

Class Association: Sonar Class Association, P.O. Box 3248, Darien, CT 06820.

Manufacturer: Ross Marine, Inc., 44 Pasture Lane, Darien, CT 06820. 203/655-4548

SPECIFICATIONS:
SONAR
LOA: 23'
DWL: 18.75'
Beam: 7.8'
Draft: 3.9'
Weight: 2100 lbs.
Sail Area: 250 s.f.

Approximate Price:
Upon request.

SONAR

RAVEN

The forerunner of this popular class was designed in the late 1940's by Roger McAleer. Construction in fiberglass began in 1951, which boosted popularity. There are approximately 300 registered boats with active fleets in many eastern states.

Many **RAVENS** are used only for pleasure sailing. She is a large daysailer with a lot of moving around room. **RAVEN** has comfortable seating. Her cockpit runs well forward, allowing spinnaker setting without climbing

RAVEN

out on deck. Trailering is no problem with this center-board boat weighing approximately 1200 lbs.

RAVEN is fast. This big daysailer is a modern planing hull and has been touted as one of the fastest in the world.

Class Association: Raven Class, 3500 Bluff Court, Godfrey, IL 62035.

Manufacturer: Cape Cod Shipbuilding Co., Narrows Road, Box 152, Wareham, MA 02571. 617/295-3550

SPECIFICATIONS:
RAVEN
LOA: 24'3"
LWL: 21'1"
Beam: 7'
Draft:
 board up 7"
 board down 5'4"
Weight (min):
 1170 lbs.

Approximate
Price: $15,843.

For Our Supply Department

O God of the Market Place, we commend to Thee for special blessings the personnel who work in the ship's stores and in the Supply Department. May we not take for granted their labors in caring for our needs. May we remind ourselves that all men must appear before Thee for final inventory. In that day, we pray that our books will be in good order. Amen.

INTERNATIONAL SOLING

Designed by Jan H. Linge in the early 1960's, the **SOLING** gained fame quickly. In 1968, the first year of production, over 360 had been built and she had been chosen as a class for the 1972 Olympics. National and international class associations had also been founded. By 1984, approximately 4000 **SOLINGS** had been built and 22 nations were competing in the Olympics. She has been in all the Olympics since.

The **SOLING** isn't normally thought of as a trainer, but does lack some of the physical requirements for crew of most of her smaller Olympic counterparts. She does not emphasize boat speed or crew acrobatics, but rather a happy medium, emphasizing the more subtle aspects of winning.

These are sturdy keelboats that will hold up for many years and can be sailed in heavy weather. Many championships are won in older boats. The **SOLING** is

INTERNATIONAL SOLING

beautiful on the water and is an excellent club racer or individual pleasure/racing boat.

Class Association: Canada - Mrs. Joanne L. Abbott, Treasurer, 1803 Modeland Rd., Sarnia, Ontario, Canada N7S 5M7.

Class Association: USA - U.S. Soling Association, Larry Booth, President, 220 E. Clovernook Lane, Fox Point, WI 53217.

Manufacturer: Abbott Boats, Ltd., 1458 London Road, Sarnia, Ontario, Canada N7S 1P7. 519/542-2771.

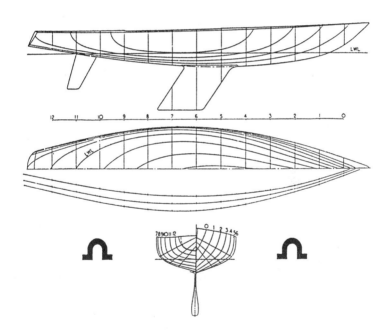

SPECIFICATIONS: SOLING
LOA: 26'11", LWL: 20', Beam: 6'3", Draft: 4'3", Displacement: 2200 lbs., Sail Area: 233 s.f.

Approximate Price: $14,000.

E SCOW

The **E SCOW** is a beautiful, well-balanced and competitive high performance racer in the lakes and bays of the U.S. Many of the world's best known sailors from the ranks of dinghies to ocean racers name the **E SCOW** as one of their all-time favorites.

Designed to race with 3 or 4 people, the **E SCOW** has all the modern gear (including spinnaker) to keep the crew working as a team in order to provide the exhilarating ride for which she is known.

The **E SCOW** was the third one-design accepted by the Inland Lake Yachting Association, way back in 1928. The class continues to enjoy a strong national organization that, in cooperation with the ILYA, governs its rules.

E SCOW

Class Association: Inland Lake Yachting Association, P.O. Box 311, Fontana, Wisconsin 53125. 414/275-6921

Class Association: National Class "E" Scow Association, 122 Laurel Avenue, Toms River, NJ 08753.

Manufacturer: Melges Boat Works, Inc., Zenda, Wisconsin 53195. 414/248-6621

Manufacturer: Johnson Boat Works, 4495 Lake Avenue, White Bear Lake, MN 55110. 612/429-7221

SPECIFICATIONS
E SCOW
LOA: 28'
Beam: 6'9"
Sail Area:
  Main 228 s.f.
  Jib 95 s.f.
  Spinnaker 550 s.f.
Hull Wt.: 965 lbs.

Approx. Price:
$13,000-$13,655

Dedication of a Recreation Room

Eternal God, our Father, we have assembled ourselves to dedicate this space as the Crew's Recreation Room. We thank Thee for service in a Command which is mindful of the needs of the crew. Grant, O Lord, that all who enter herein may find rest and joyful fellowship. Help us to keep it clean with sound manners and unsoiled speech. May the use of this compartment bring a will and a strength to go about our duties as free men in defense of a free land. Amen.

INTERNATIONAL DRAGON

The **INTERNATIONAL DRAGON** is a keel boat of traditional Scandinavian design...good looking, fine sailing and sea kindly. Designed in 1928 as a racing sailboat that the crew could live aboard during the regattas, the **DRAGON** immediately became popular in the Scandinavian countries. Her worldwide popularity established the yacht as an Olympic class in 1948, a status maintained through 1972. Today, numbering nearly 4500 yachts, the **DRAGON** has grown to be the world's largest one-design displacement keel boat.

Continually updated through the years, the modern **DRAGON** is in every respect an up to the minute racer. Today's boat is a 3740 lb. yacht of wood or fiberglass. Spars are wood or primarily aluminum. She is close winded in light air, excels in heavy air and rough seas, is safe to sail and easy to handle. The yacht is primarily a racing machine, crewed by three, but can be sailed easily single-handed and is a pleasurable daysailer.

The **DRAGON** class is a strict one-design class, rigidly controlled by the International Yacht Racing Union; the yachts must meet detailed specifications of material, measurement and weight. These regulations insure that any well maintained and well sailed **DRAGON** will be competitive with all others, regardless of age.

Over 290 **DRAGONS** are registered in the U.S. and over 135 in Canada. Fleets compete in Rochester, Cleveland and Seattle in the U.S. and Ottawa, Toronto and Vancouver in Canada, plus inter-fleet events world-wide.

Class Association: American International Dragon Association, 787 Mendon-Ionia Road, Ionia, NY 14475.

SPECIFICATIONS: DRAGON
LOA: 29'4", LWL: 18'8", Beam: 6'5", Draft: 3'11", Sail Area: Main & Genoa - 300 s.f., Spinnaker - 300 s.f., Weight: 3740 lbs.

Approximate Price: $25,000

INTERNATIONAL DRAGON

INTERNATIONAL 210

Ray Hunt designed the **INTERNATIONAL 210** in 1945 as a comfortable, safe, family daysailer/racer, after several people inquired about a larger boat than the **110**, based on the same principles.

During that same year, a group of yacht clubs in Massachusetts Bay was looking for a good inter-club racer. They wanted a boat for under $1500. The boat had to be good for racing as well as pleasant for daysailing. She had to be a modern boat that will always be uniform so it couldn't be out-built. They chose Ray Hunt's 210.

The Class Association was founded in 1946 and they grew rapidly. Over 437 of these beauties have been built. Presently, there are approximately 80 boats actively racing but the Class Association reports a comeback is taking place as interest in these older classes is increasing.

These sleek, classical daysailers are beautiful on the water. The **210** races with a crew of 3 or 4 and can be day-sailed with more.

Class Association: International 210 Association, Kathy Klok, Publicity, 5565 Linda Lane, Kalamazoo, MI 49004.

Manufacturer: Obscure Boats, Inc., P.O. Box 474, Newport, RI 02840. 401/846-6166

SPECIFICATIONS:
INTERNATIONAL 210
LOA: 29'9 5/8"
Beam: 5'10"
Draft: 3'10"
Displacement: 2300 lbs.
Ballast: 1175 lbs.

**Approximate
Price: $18,000**

INTERNATIONAL 210
Photo by: Kathy Klok

SHIELDS

Many believe the **SHIELDS** to be the finest all-around fiberglass, keel, one-design racing and daysailing yacht now afloat.

In looks and performance, the **SHIELDS** is entirely worthy of her distinguished heritage. The idea for her creation originated with Cornelius Shields, one of America's most eminent racing yachtsmen and dedicated enthusiasts responsible for the consecutive successes on Long Island Sound of the Sound Interclub and International One-Design Classes.

322

SHIELDS

The **SHIELDS** Class concept of an ideal, moderately sized, low maintenance, high performance, open cockpit, keel-ballasted sailboat was translated under Olin Stephen's personal supervision into plans and specifications by the New York firm of Sparkman & Stephens, designers of many America's Cup defenders.

Working together, they developed the concept of a one-design which would bring out the very best of a competitive sailor's ability. Every detail was scrupulously studied and developed before being incorporated into the final Sparkman & Stephens design.

Years of growth under the direction of Mr. Shields, and the Class Association have upheld the concept of the **SHIELDS** as a "One-Design" Class. The strict by-laws prevent annual rule changes, thereby enabling those on a limited budget to sail competitively year after year. There are 17 fleets in the U.S.

Class Association: Shields Class Association, Kelly M. McSweeny, P.O. Box 515, Marion, MA 02738.

Manufacturer: Cape Cod Shipbuilding Co., Wareham, MA 02571. 617/295-3550

SPECIFICATIONS:
SHIELDS
LOA: 30'2.5"
LWL: 20'
Beam: 6'5.25"
Sail Area: 360 s.f.
Draft: 4'9"
Ballast: 3080 lbs.
Displacement:
4600 lbs.

**Approximate
Price:** $24,000.

ETCHELLS 22 (E-22)

The **E-22** is a big, fast, simple, stable and sleek racing sloop that can be sailed competitively and in comfort by three average, everyday sailors in all conditions. She is a brilliant performer and can tack in 70 degrees. With a low wetted surface hullform, she keeps moving in the slightest breeze. In 20+ knots of wind, the **E-22** absolutely flies.

Her simplicity includes a small sailplan and a basic rig, which is easy to manage. There is a marked absence of sophisticated mast mechanisms, complex sail controls and deck gadgetry. She is certainly not dominated by unneeded gear.

She is extremely stiff and stable. A 63% ballast/displacement ratio and high form stability minimizes the effect of crew weight. No broaching, no hiking, no fatigue. Sailors of both sexes and all ages are equally competitive. Family crews can sail together and win.

ETCHELLS 22 (E-22)

The E-22 is a strong, established and well administered one-design class, which provides high quality racing on a club, regional or international basis. The boats can be trailered, however, crews often enjoy traveling with their own sails to regattas in borrowed or chartered boats. Racing is always close.

She is easy to own -- easy to maintain (no wood), light enough to dry sail, can be trailered (no yard bills), easy to rig and unrig, and easy to manage. E-22's are a good investment. Control of construction by the class association and the IYRU insures quality and uniformity. Every E-22 ever made is still competitive. These boats hold exceptional resale value.

Despite her size, she is not a racer/cruiser, cruiser/racer, offshore one-design, or mini yacht. No sail changes, no genoas, no reefing, no rating rules, no galley time, no bunks & linen, no electrical gear, no motor, no hydraulics, no obsolescence.

Class Association: International E-22 Class Association, Box 534 Wall Street Station, New York, NY 10268.

Manufacturer: Ontario Yachts, 243 Speers Road, Oakville, Ontario, Canada L6K 2E8.   416/845-1153

SPECIFICATIONS:
ETCHELLS 22 (E-22)
LOA: 30'6"
LWL: 22'
Beam: 6'11.5"
Draft: 4'6"
Weight: 3400 lbs.
Sail Area: 291 s.f.
Spinnaker: 400 s.f.

Approximate
Price: $21,920

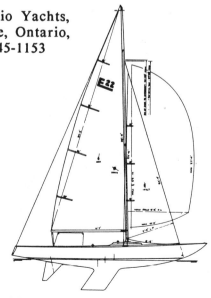

ATLANTIC

A sweet, easy boat to sail, the **ATLANTIC** Coast one-designs are one of the largest, fastest and best-known of the one-design daysailing yachts. She is among W Starling Burgess' most popular racing models (he also designed **"Ranger"**, the **J-Class** defender for the America's Cup). Surprisingly fast in light weather, yet extraordinarily steady, she's safe and seaworthy in strong winds and rough seas. Due to her deep 2200 pound lead keel reefing is seldom necessary and is unknown in racing practice.

She carries a Marconi main sail, a good sized loose-footed jib and a moderately large spinnaker. She can do six and a half knots without planing. With an adjustable backstay, efficient running rigging, perfect balance and large open cockpit, she can easily be handled by a crew of two in moderate weather, although she is usually seen with three to five aboard.

Founded in 1929, the Atlantic Class Association cautiously and jealously guards the strict one-design features of this class. In 1954, they voted to have the **ATLANTICS** built exclusively by Cape Cod Shipbuilding Co., who has specialized in fiberglass boat construction since 1945.

Class Association: Atlantic Class Association, 25? Milbank Avenue, Greenwich, CT 06830.

Manufacturer: Cape Cod Shipbuilding Co., Wareham Massachusetts 02571. 617/295-3550

SPECIFICATIONS: ATLANTIC
LOA: 30'7", LWL: 21'6", Beam: 6'6", Draft: 4'9", Weight 4559 lbs., Lead Keel: 2200 lbs., Sail Area: Main - 276 s.f. Jib - 100 s.f., Spinnaker - 210 s.f.

Approximate Price: $25,947.

INTERNATIONAL ONE DESIGN

This classic beauty was born on Long Island Sound in 1936, and now has fleets in the U.S., British Isles, Scandinavia and Bermuda.

She's a magnificent reminder of yachting's "golden age". The **INTERNATIONAL ONE DESIGN** was designed by Bjarne Aas of Norway, who was commissioned by Corny Shields to produce a 33 foot version of the Bermudian 6-Meter, **Saga**. She carries the meter-boat look of long, narrow hull with long overhangs, deep draft and graceful sheer. She slices through the water, is balanced perfectly and a delight to sail.

INTERNATIONAL ONE DESIGNS produced today are fiberglass. This has not changed her performance, a

328

INTERNATIONAL ONE DESIGN

the class association supervised the mold construction using a wooden hull as a pattern. Glass boats race evenly with their older wooden sisters. The class is devoted to true one-design philosophy, even to the point of making sail purchases en bloc. Group purchase of sails, masts and other equipment has resulted in great savings to individual owners. This class is assuring there is no such thing as a "checkbook champion" in the class.

Class Association: International One Design, Edward D. Cook, Jr., 32 Flint Street, Marblehead, MA 01945.

Manufacturer: Able Marine, Clark Point Road, P.O. Box 25, Southwest Harbor, ME 04679. 207/244-5135

SPECIFICATIONS: INTERNATIONAL ONE DESIGN
LOA: 33'5", LWL: 21'5", Beam: 6'9", Draft: 5'6", Sail Area: 466 s.f., Displacement: 7120 lbs., Ballast: 4100 lbs.
Approximate Price: $30,000.

A SCOW

Developed in the 1890's, the **A SCOW** is the largest, fastest and most powerful of all the scows. It has enjoyed a resurgence in competitive racing since being retooled in 1979. Although the same basic size and shape as the original 1890 boats, like the rest of the scows, it is now made of fiberglass and has all modern, sophisticated rigging and gear needed to make this incredible boat perform and last for years.

Clocked at over 25 mph, this *"rocketship"* is not for novices. It requires a practiced crew of six to handle this ultimate scow. It is also possible to provide an unforgettable pleasure ride for 8-10 people.

The **A SCOW** is one of the classes of boats making up the Inland Lake Yachting Association (ILYA), one of

A SCOW

the strongest sailing associations in the world. It was formed in 1898 and consists of approximately 50 clubs and over 4000 sailors.

Class Association: Inland Lake Yachting Association, P.O. Box 311, Fontana, Wisconsin 53125. 414/275-6921

Manufacturer: Melges Boat Works, Inc., Zenda, Wisconsin 53195. 414/248-6621

SPECIFICATIONS:
A SCOW
LOA: 38'
Beam: 8'
Hull Weight: 1850 lbs.
Sail Area:
  Main 350 s.f.
  Jib 150 s.f.
  Spinnaker 1200 s.f.

Approximate Price: $24,000.

O Thou, who can satisfy the yearnings of our hearts, draw nigh unto us as we seek rest for the night. We have so many needs, and the questions of why and how are often upon our lips. We are driven by the winds of fortune and chance, and we are tempted to sail alone. Yet, when we are quite and count our blessings, we know that all things work for good to those who love Thee. We rest at peace with our shipmates and ourselves because Thou art near. Amen.

UNITED STATES
YACHT RACING UNION

UNITED STATES YACHT RACING UNION

The United States Yacht Racing Union -- **USYRU** is America's national sailing association.

Founded in 1897 to unify the sport of sailboat racing, **USYRU** has grown into a nationwide organization that serves every kind of sailing. The National Sports Act of 1978 established **USYRU** as the official governing body for sailing in the U.S.

USYRU is a nonprofit organization, run by and for sailors themselves. From beginners to world champions, boardsailors to maxi-boat skippers, individual sailors are the heart of **USYRU**.

USYRU serves as an umbrella organization for most of the one-design classes listed in this book, with programs that range from class promotion to regatta organization and insurance.

USYRU's growing list of services to individual sailors includes a subscription to the monthly magazine **AMERICAN SAILOR** . . . free copies of the racing rulebook, appeals updates, and USYRU yearbook . . . and discounts on sailing books, services, and travel.

USYRU's exclusive low-cost member boat loans can even help put you into one of the dinghies or daysailers listed in this book.

For more information, call **USYRU** at (401) 849-5200, or write: USYRU, Box 209, Newport, RI 02840.

First-year dues are only $25 ($40 Family, $10 under 21). Dues can be charged to your VISA or MasterCard by calling toll-free 1-800-327-0303.

APPENDIX

Portsmouth Yardstick

The Portsmouth Yardstick is a widely used method of rating boats of different classes racing on the same course. The rating is derived from actual racing experience. By comparing Portsmouth numbers, one can get an idea of relative speed potential of the boat/class. The lower the number, the faster the boat should be.

The numbers listed are the Basic Portsmouth Numbers (D-PN) and are good for comparison. Parentheses "( )" around numbers indicate that these numbers are based on a limited amount of race data (5 to 15 data points) and are suspect. Brackets "[ ]" around numbers indicate that these numbers are based on estimates from less than 5 data points or have been calculated from other rating systems formulae. Bracketed numbers are highly suspect and individual clubs are urged to verify and modify them with their own race data.

D-PN works well for classes with similar characteristics and rig where wind velocity is not a factor. D-PN may be used to separate handicap classes into fleets or to establish fleets for level class racing. Race committees faced with a large entry in mixed fleet racing on water where marked changes in wind conditions are common may find D-PN the preferred method for handicapping. In actual practice, race committees can adjust these numbers up or down for wind conditions and other factors. For a complete listing of Portsmouth Numbers, contact the United States Yacht Racing Union.

Centerboard Boats	D-PN
International 14	87.4
International 420	97.5
International 470	86.9
International 505	80.5
A Scow	62.1
Aqua Finn	[105.2]
Beetle Cat	102.8
Blue Jay	109.2
Buccaneer 18	88.4
Butterfly	108.3
C Scow	80.3

Capri 14.2	(107.2)
CL 14	104.9
CL 16	96.6
International Contender	91.6
Coronado 15	91.7
Cyclone 13	98.2
Day Sailer 3	100.0
Dolphin 17	96.2
Dolphin Super Senior	106.8
Doughdish	[105.0]
Dyer Dinghy	(110.8)
E Scow	74.0
Finn	92.6
Fireball	86.0
International FJ	98.3
International Flying Dutchman	80.0
Flying Scot	90.4
Force 5	96.0
Galilee 15	[99.4]
Gemini	98.2
Highlander	85.0
Holder 12	97.0
Holder 14 MKII	(106.1)
Holder Hawk	[113.0]
Johnson J Sailer	93.5
Johnson Mini-Scow	[110.0]
Knockabout	[95.0]
Laser	92.3
Laser II	91.7
Laser Radial	(96.5)
Lido 14	100.
Lightning	89.5
M-16 Scow	90.9
M 20 Scow	83.7
MC Scow	91.3
Mercury Sloop	[117.0]
Mirror Dinghy	117.3
Mistral 4.04	(96.0)
Mistral 4.7	[95.6]
Mistral 15	[98.5]
Mistral 16	[96.5]
Mobjack	91.4
Montgomery 6-8	[135.0]

Montgomery 7-11	[134.0]
International Moth	108.6
Optimist Pram	[138.0]
Penguin	112.6
Precision 16	99.1
Puffer	111.5
Raven	82.6
Rhodes 18	102.0
Rhodes 19	96.3
Sea Devil	[112.0]
Sea Pearl 21	(99.6)
Sea Snark	130.0
Sea Witch	110.4
Snipe	93.6
Sundancer	[128.0]
Sunfish	104.8
Super Ray 17	[83.0]
Super Snark	[134.0]
Teal	99.7
Tern	(122.0)
The Ten	114.7
The Twelve	(96.4)
Thistle	83.0
Town Class	96.9
Wayfarer	91.7
Windmill	89.9
X-Boat (Class X)	97.7
Y-Flyer	88.4

Keel Boats	D-PN
International 210	87.0
Bull's Eye	116.1
International Dragon	89.5
Etchell's 22 (E-22)	(76.6)
Mercury Class Yacht	(102.7)
Mercury Sloop	[116.0]
Rhodes 19	97.3
Shields	(83.8)
International Soling	82.0
Star	83.5
Yngling	94.0

APPENDIX
PHRF Handicaps

PHRF Handicap is a "seconds-per-mile" handicap system, which also allows different classes to compete on the same course. The handicap is multiplied by the course distance in miles to give the "time allowance" for the race. Corrected time is simply "finish time" minus "time allowance".

PHRF Handicaps can vary slightly from area to area. The handicaps listed below were calculated by averaging all areas reporting handicaps to the United States Yacht Racing Union. For a complete listing of PHRF Handicaps, contact the USYRU.

Boat Name	PHRF Handicap
Atlantic	159
International Dragon	203
E-22 (Etchells 22)	123
Highlander	200
Impulse 21	173
International One Design	152
Lightning	180
Rhodes 19	262
Sandpiper	300
International Soling	153
Sonar	174
Star	146
X 21	240
Yngling	232

GLOSSARY

Basic definitions of words and terms are given according to their use in this book. No attempt is made to give complete definitions.

Aft Towards, near, at or behind the stern.

Backstay A wire supporting the mast to stop forward movement.

Bail To remove water from the boat.

Ballast Weight placed low in a boat to provide stability, usually metal.

Beam Width of a boat at its widest point.

Boom vang A line secured to the boom to hold it down.

Boom A spar used to extend the foot of a sail.

Bow The forward end of a boat.

Bowsprit A spar which projects forward past the bow, in order to extend the sail area of the forward sail.

Cat-rigged A rig used for small boats, consisting of one large sail.

Centerboard A pivoting plate lowered through a slot in the center of the hull to reduce sideways sliding.

Chine A line running along the side of a boat, where the bottom forms an angle to the side.

Class A general category into which boats of the same, or similar, design are placed.

Clew The aftermost corner of a triangular sail. Either lower corner on a spinnaker.

Coaming A vertical extension above the deck which prevents water from entering the cockpit.

Cockpit The after-well (sunken space) in a small boat, used for the helmsman and crew.

Cuddy A locker in a small open boat.

Cuddy cabin An open cabin at forward or aft in a small boat, used mainly for storage.

Cunningham A control device for the mainsail, which uses a line to pull the mainsail down a short distance from the luff to the tack. It flattens the sail.

Daggerboard A board dropped vertically through the center of the hull. When lowered it performs as a keel. Can be removed for beaching or sailing downwind.

Daysailer A sailboat used for pleasure sailing and/or racing. Not usually equipped with a cabin suitable for extended overnight stays (thus, the name "daysailer").

Dinghy An open boat, equipped with oars, or sail, or motor, or a combination of these. Dinghies are used for pleasure sailing, racing and as tender and lifeboat on a larger boat.

Displacement The weight of the water displaced by a floating boat. Displacement is the same as the weight of the boat itself.

Dory A small flat-bottomed open boat, originally used primarily by fishermen for setting their lines. Modified sailing dories are still being built for pleasure sailing.

Double-ender A boat which has a pointed bow and stern.

Downhaul A line used to haul a sail down, particularly the mainsail.

Draft The depth of water which a ship requires to float freely. The depth of a boat from the water line to the lowest point of the hull.

Fairlead A ringbolt, eye or loop, which is used to guide ropes in the required direction.

Fiberglass Glass reinforced plastic; material used for boat building.

Foot The lower edge of a sail.

Fore Towards, near or at the bow.

Fore-and-aft In line from the bow to the stern; on, or parallel to, the centerline.

Foresail Triangular shaped sail set before the mast.

Forestay A line (stay) leading from the masthead to the bow, to keep the mast from falling backwards.

Fractional rig A design in which the forestay does not go to the top of the mast, only a fraction of the way, such as 3/4, 7/8, etc.

Freeboard The portion of a boat's hull which is not submerged in water.

Gaff A spar which extends the head of a four-sided fore-and-aft mainsail (gaff rig).

Gaff rig A four-sided fore-and-aft sail extended by two spars, a gaff and a boom, which has its forward side or luff pivoting about a mast to which it is attached.

Genoa A large, triangular foresail, which extends aft behind the mast. Used in cruising and racing, when reaching.

Gunnel Same as gunwale.

Gunter rig A rig in which the gaff slides up a mast to form an extension to the mast.

Gunwale The upper edge of the side of the hull. Pronunciation "gunnel".

Halyard A line for hoisting sails.

Heeling attitude A position of a boat when it lies over at an angle.

Helm The steering mechanism of a boat.

Helmsman One who steers.

Hiking stick An extension of the tiller, allowing the helmsman to sit at a distance from the tiller.

Hiking strap Fore and aft straps attached to the boat, allowing crew members to hook their feet when hiking out.

Hull The body of a boat, exclusive of masts, sails, rigging, machinery, equipment, etc.

ILYA Inland Lake Yachting Association.

IYRU International Yacht Racing Union.

Jib A fore-and-aft sail, triangular in shape. It is set forward of the mast and is also called a headsail.

Keel The fixed underwater part of a sail boat, used to prevent sideways drift. Provides stability.

Kick-up A rudder or centerboard that rotates back and up when an obstacle comes in contact with it. Used when beaching.

Lapstrake A term applied to boats in which the strakes (boards or planks) are overlapping. The top strake lays over the outside of the strake below.

Lee, leeward The area away from the wind, downwind. Being in the lee of an object is being sheltered by it.

Leeboard Boards attached vertically to the outside of the hull to prevent leeway.

Leech Both side edges of a square sail, or the afteredge of a fore-and-aft sail.

Leeway Distance between the course steered by a boat and that actually run. Also called "drift".

LOA Length overall. The length of a boat, from the furthest point fore to the furthest point aft.

Luff The forward edge of a sail; (2) to bring the boat's head closer to the wind; (3) to luff up is to turn the boat's head into the wind.

LWL Length water line. With a boat sitting in the water, the distance fore-to-aft of where it touches the water.

Main A word to distinguish the principal parts or places on a boat.

Mainsail The largest sail set from the main mast.

Marconi rig A modern sailing rig with a triangular mainsail.

Mast A pole, or system of poles, used to support the sails.

Mast step A recess, fitting, or construction into which the bottom of the mast is placed.

Masthead The top of the mast.

Masthead rig A rig design where the forestay runs to the peak of the mast.

Oarlock A support which holds the oar in place.

One design A boat built to conform to rules so that it is identical, or nearly identical, to others in the same class.

Outhaul A line used to pull the clew of the mainsail towards the end of the boom.

PHRF See Appendix.

Port The left hand side of a boat, when looking forward.

Portsmouth yardstick See Appendix.

Rating A method of measuring dimensions or performance of boats of different sizes and shapes, so they can race on a handicap basis, such as Portsmouth or PHRF. **Rig** The manner in which a boat's mast, spars and sails are arranged.

Roach The curved leech of a sail.

Roller reefing Reducing the area of a sail by rolling it around the boom, mast or stay.

Rub-rail The beading running around the outside of a boat, just beneath the gunwale, to protect it against damage when touching other boats or objects. Usually constructed of wood, rubber or plastic.

Rudder A movable, underwater device used for steering a boat. Usually made of wood or metal.

Running rigging The portion of the rigging used to control sails and equipment. Ropes which hoist and sheet sails.

Scow A flat bottomed boat, with sloping ends. The bow and stern are square across instead of coming to a point. Some have the same width fore and aft, while some narrow slightly towards the ends.

Seat locker A storage locker located under the cockpit seat.

Self-bailing cockpit Watertight cockpit with drains, scuppers, or bailers which remove water.

Shackle A U-shaped link with a bolt, used to connect links and eyes.

Sheer A straight or curved line, which the deck line of a boat makes when viewed from the side.

Sheet A rope fastened to one or both of the lower corners of a sail. Used to extend it or to change its direction.

Shrouds Wires supporting the mast on either side. Also called "standing rigging".

Skeg The projecting section of the underwater surface of a boat where the rudder is hung.

Sloop, sloop rig A single-masted boat, with only one headsail. Can be gaff-rigged or Marconi-rigged.

Spars A term used for masts, booms, gaffs and bowsprits.

Spinnaker A large, baggy, loose-footed triangular sail. Used when cruising or racing, when running before the wind.

Spreaders Struts attached to the mast on either side to increase the speed and holding power of the main shrouds. Also called "cross-trees".

Sprit rig, sprit sail A boat rigged with a quadrilateral sail extended by a spar reaching from the mast to the upper aftercorner of the sail.

Standing rigging Shrouds and stays which support the mast.

Starboard The right-hand side of the boat looking forward.

Stays The parts of the standing rigging which support the mast in a fore-and-aft direction.

Stem The upright post or bar of the bow. Made of wood or metal.

Stern The afterpart (rear) of a boat.

Tabernacle A hinged mast step, which is located on deck.

Tack (1) The bottom forward corner on a triangular sail; (2) to turn the bow of a boat through the wind, so that it blows across the opposite side.

Tender A small boat used for transporting people and stores to a yacht or other larger boat.

Tiller An attachment to the rudder, by which the rudder is controlled. Usually made of wood or metal.

Trapeze A support used by crew members of a racing boat, enabling them to place their weight further outboard thus helping to keep the boat level.

Traveler A slide which travels on a track, and is used for changing sheet angles.

Uphaul A line used to raise a spinnaker pole, or other objects.

USYRU United States Yacht Racing Union.

Vang A line used to keep a gaff or sprit from sagging. Also called "guy".

Whisker pole A spar used to push the clew of the jib away from the boat when running downwind.

Yacht tender A small boat used for transporting people and stores to a yacht.

ORDER FORM

Barca De Vela Publishing
Post Office Box 37168-W
Phoenix, AZ 85069-7168 USA
Telephone 602/864-9493

Please send me **DINGHIES AND DAYSAILERS** by Butch
& Rita Wilcox.

_____ Copies @ $14.95 each   Total $_____

Arizona Residents add 5% sales tax.   _____

Shipping: $1 for the first book and
75 cents for each additional book.   _____

TOTAL $_____

I understand that I may return the book for a full
refund if not satisfied.

Name:_____

Address:_____

_____Zip:_____

_____ I can't wait 3-4 weeks for Book Rate. Here is
$3.00 per book for Priority Mail.

ORDER FORM

Barca De Vela Publishing
Post Office Box 37168-W
Phoenix, AZ 85069-7168 USA
Telephone 602/864-9493

Please send me **DINGHIES AND DAYSAILERS** by Butch & Rita Wilcox.

_____ Copies @ $14.95 each   Total $_____

Arizona Residents add 5% sales tax.   _____

Shipping: $1 for the first book and
75 cents for each additional book.   _____

TOTAL $_____

I understand that I may return the book for a full refund if not satisfied.

Name:_____

Address:_____

_____Zip:_____

_____   I can't wait 3-4 weeks for Book Rate. Here is
         $3.00 per book for Priority Mail.

NOTES

NOTES

J/

1